SPIRITUAL
FRIENDSHIP

Finding Love in the Church
as a Celibate Gay Christian

WESLEY HILL

Brazos Press
a division of Baker Publishing Group
Grand Rapids, Michigan

Published by Brazos Press
a division of Baker Publishing Group
P.O. Box 6287, Grand Rapids, MI 49516-6287
www.brazospress.com

Printed in the United States of America

.

Library of Congress Cataloging-in-Publication Data
Hill, Wesley, 1981–
    Spiritual friendship : finding love in the church as a celibate gay Christian
    / Wesley Hill.
        pages cm
    ISBN 978-1-58743-349-8 (pbk.)
    1. Friendship—Religious aspects—Christianity. 2. Single people—Conduct
of life. I. Title.
    BV4647.F7H55 2015
    241′.6762—dc23   2014037652

16   17   18   19   20   21   22   8   7   6   5   4   3   2

"Wesley Hill's courageous, thought-provoking book seeks to recover 'friendship as a genuine love in its own right.' At one level, it is a historically rooted and theologically nuanced essay that opens up fresh perspectives on a topic that is crucial but too rarely pondered. But at another level, *Spiritual Friendship* belongs to the classic genre of Christian confessional autobiography, a genre that can be traced back to St. Augustine; it is both searing in its honesty and moving in its chastened hope for grace."

—**Richard B. Hays**, Duke Divinity School

"This is a remarkable book. Drawing on a deep reservoir of biblical wisdom and theological imagination, Wesley Hill explores the possibilities for a truly Christian picture of friendship. And because this exploration requires him to think also about how his friendship both contributes to and differs from the fellowship that all Christians share, he makes here a significant contribution to the general theology of the church as well."

—**Alan Jacobs**, Honors College, Baylor University

"Medieval monks expressed their love for one another with what to us is cringe-inducing intimacy, and not so long ago Christians still entered formal bonds of friendship by taking vows that sound like marriage vows. We don't do that anymore, with our commitment to uncommitted freedom, our turnover habits, our sexualization of everything and everyone, and our resignation to loneliness. Wesley Hill's very personal book is an elegant, theologically rich plea on behalf of the love of friendship that uncovers fresh ways to improvise on a lost Christian tradition of committed spiritual friendship."

—**Peter Leithart**, president, Theopolis Institute, Birmingham, Alabama

"*Spiritual Friendship* weaves together Scripture, Christian history, art, and personal experience. This is a portrait, not a treatise. It depicts friendship's flaws and failures but also shows how friendship can bear spiritual fruit and help us build up the kingdom of God. Wesley Hill challenges us all to strengthen our own friendships and those around us, and offers guidance in these tasks from his own experience and from the Christian past."

—**Eve Tushnet**, author of *Gay and Catholic: Accepting My Sexuality, Finding Community, Living My Faith*

"With disarming frankness, Wesley Hill charts the loss of friendship from our world and mounts a compelling case for its recovery as a communally celebrated form of Christian love. Hill's is a voice that needs to be heard. His book is a powerful challenge to the contemporary church as well as a profound meditation on the difficult, wonderful, risky business of loving and being loved."

—**Benjamin Myers**, Charles Sturt University, Sydney, Australia

"In a highly engaging and very accessible manner, Hill uses examples from art, literature, film, and especially his own life to explore what in our culture today most endangers friendship, how Christianity redefines our understanding of friendship, and how our churches can be the best settings for nurturing the faithful, challenging, and blessed relationships Hill presents to us. *Spiritual Friendship* is a timely gift the reader will quickly take to heart."

—**Paul J. Wadell**, St. Norbert College; author of *Becoming Friends: Worship, Justice, and the Practice of Christian Friendship*

"This book is a rare find! Hill eloquently speaks into one of the great spiritual crises of our day: the meaning of love and specifically of friendship in Christ. This courageous personal and theological account of friendship will both challenge and illuminate those seeking to renew the church's witness today."

—**J. Todd Billings**, Western Theological Seminary, Holland, Michigan

"Wesley Hill captured my imagination by presenting a vision of friendship—spiritual friendship—that has been our Christian heritage. Each of us who make up the body of Christ will be enriched and our corporate witness to a broader culture enhanced if we can find a way to live into this vision."

—**Mark A. Yarhouse**, Regent University

"Too gay for some and too chaste for others, for many Wesley Hill is not supposed to exist. But exist he does, even to flourishing. Challenging settled convictions on all sides of the sexuality debate, he testifies here—alongside countless celibate Christians before him—to the richness of intimate friendships that dare violate our society's sole remaining commandment: 'Thou shalt have sex.'"

—**Matthew Milliner**, Wheaton College

For Mike, Chris J., David, Abraham,
Jono, Orrey, and Aidan

In memory of Chris M.

At points of their highest significance, at
their peaks, the two currents, brotherhood
and friendship, strive to merge fully.

—Pavel Florensky

[John Henry Newman and Ambrose St. John's] love was not the less intense for being spiritual. Perhaps, it was the more so.

—Alan Bray

Contents

Author's Note

This book is a work of theological, historical, cultural, and spiritual reflection, but I've included elements of memoir as well. The personal stories I tell are all true, but in some cases I have changed the names and identifying details of people I mention. Where I've used real names, I've received permission to do so. In at least one of the stories, I've created a composite character, conflating several experiences with different friends into one narrative. In the case of emails, I've quoted them verbatim, and I've fact-checked the conversations I report. Any errors are, of course, my own.

Introduction

This book began, I suppose, like many writing projects do—with a question that wouldn't leave me alone. At the time I started thinking of writing, I was reading many celebrations of friendship. Some of these writings were from decades ago, and some were hot off the press. Some were written by Christians, others by people from different faiths or no faith at all. But one thing they all seemed to agree on was that friendship is the freest, the least constrained, the least fixed and determined, of all human loves. Try as you might, you can't ever stop being a father or a mother. You may try to disown your parents, but you can't quit being a daughter or a son. You may divorce your spouse, but that won't change your status as an ex-wife or an ex-husband. And although you may believe you're acting coolly and rationally when you stride across the bar to flirt with a potential date, most people would describe that experience as one of being compelled or swept up by passions outside your direct control. But friendship, it is usually said—in contrast to all these varying degrees of relational obligation—stands apart. Unlike romantic relationships or the bonds between siblings, friendship is entirely *voluntary*, uncoerced, and unencumbered by any sense of duty or debt. And friendship is thereby rendered special, mysterious, and deeply rewarding; it is, as C. S. Lewis describes it, "the least instinctive, organic, biological, gregarious and necessary." We may choose to end a friendship at any time—that's the prerogative this particular form of love affords us. But precisely for that reason, friendship is uniquely precious: our friends are the ones we've chosen, the elected few.

This book began with my doubts about that claim—or, maybe more precisely, my worry over what that claim, assuming it's true, means for our practice of friendship. If friendship is in fact so tenuous, hanging only by the thread of my and my friend's mutual delight, then perhaps, in the end, that's not something to be celebrated as much as it is one to be grieved and, where possible, mended. Perhaps that very freedom prevents us from exploring depths of friendship that can be attained only when we accept certain limits and constraints.

Several years ago the Catholic writer and blogger Eve Tushnet wrote a blog post that convinced me there was something to this line of thought. "My actual experience of friendship," Tushnet said, "very strongly suggests a need and desire for friendships to become, over time, understood as *given*. Viewing friendships as endlessly-renewed choices may satisfy [the one who harbors] suspicion of mere promising and obligation, but I don't think it can truly satisfy the friend." In other words, granting the point that friendship in practice is often a relationship with minimal obligations and maximal liberty—to the point where a friend might not think twice about taking a job across the country and leaving his friends behind, or where a friend might feel no qualms about naming her marriage as the cure for all her ills ("My husband is my closest friend; I would be lost without him"), little understanding how this might sound to her friends who have stood by her through thick and thin up to that point—we can still ask the question whether friendship *should* be so free and unconstrained.

This book is my effort to ask that question. Should we think of friendship as based, above all, on personal preference? Should we think of it as preserving its voluntary character and thereby vulnerable at every point to dissolution if one of the friends grows tired of or burdened by the relationship? Should we consider friendship as always freshly chosen but never incurring any substantial obligations or entailing any unbreakable bonds? Or should we instead—pursuing a rather different line of thought—consider friendship more along the lines of how we think of marriage? Should we begin to imagine friendship as more stable, permanent, and binding than we often do? Should we, in short, think of our friends more like the siblings we're stuck with, like it or not, than like our acquaintances? Should we begin to consider at least some of our friends as, in large measure, tantamount to family? And if so, what needs to change about the way we approach it and seek to maintain it? Those are the questions I want to ask and explore in the pages that follow.

Mark Slouka's 2013 novel *Brewster* tells the story of two high school kids who fall into an unlikely friendship. One of them, Jon, is introverted, halting, unsure of his place in the world. The son of German immigrants who are still grieving over his brother, Aaron, who died in childhood, Jon is adrift among his family members and his peers. Ray, meanwhile, is the iconic rebel. Face flanked by strands of long hair, he projects bravado, swagger, arrogance. And yet the proverb proves its mettle: opposites attract. The two become friends.

Things are hard at Ray's house. His father drinks. So one night he asks to sleep over at Jon's. And one night turns into two. And then three.

"He slept on a mattress on my floor," says Jon. "We'd sit up late, listening to records, then turn off the light and go right on talking—about school, about girls, about life."

Jon continues:

It's like he was hungry for it—to sit in a room just playing records, talking—like he'd never done it before. Sometimes we'd get silly—even for me—and I'd have to remind myself that this was Ray Cappicciano sitting against the wall leafing through a magazine with my stuffed gorilla behind him for a backrest, its paws draped over his shoulders, its huge dark feet propped up on either side of his hips. I don't think I thought less of him for it. I understood it was important, that some part of him needed it. I even felt proud of having him there, a little tamed, not quite so dangerous now, like an actual leopard curled at the foot of the bed.

The first time we walked up the stairs he pointed to Aaron's room and mouthed the question and I nodded and said, "Yeah," and he said, "*That* can't be easy," and I said, "Yeah."

Then Jon adds three sentences, and with them the chapter closes:

It's been years. I still hear his voice, talking to me out of the dark. It was as close to having a brother as I'll ever get.

When Jon needs a word to describe the strength and warmth of the bond he felt with Ray, he reaches for a word that signifies permanence, longevity, and indestructibility. He calls his friend Ray his "brother."

And I want to suggest that we follow his lead.

&

When I mentioned to an art historian friend that I was working on a book about friendship, he immediately started directing me to sources for my project. For instance, I learned that toward the end of the nineteenth century, scores of Princeton University students would have filed into Marquand Chapel on campus to worship beneath a stained-glass window depicting the Old Testament characters, and vowed friends, David and Jonathan. Until the chapel burned in 1920, my friend pointed out, this window would have functioned as a reminder to students to make friendship a central part of their college years. Likewise, I learned about a much earlier image of Christ and St. Menas, a sixth-century icon in which Jesus's arm is draped familiarly over Menas's shoulder: clearly a gesture that removes Christ from the realm of kingship and judgment and casts him, instead, in the recognizable role of mate or comrade. It's an image that would have spoken to ancient Christians of their need to cultivate brotherly love and would have underscored for them the christological basis and focus of that love.

But by far the most intriguing and suggestive source my friend directed me to was the icon—painted (or "written," as the Christian East puts it) many times, in many hues and variations, over the centuries—of Simon of Cyrene carrying Jesus's cross. Here, my friend said, is an image of *friendship*—Simon is, above all, a friend to Jesus at a point of dire need—and one that we might easily overlook. The story of Simon is told in the Gospels of Matthew, Mark, and Luke, but if you blink, you'll miss it. Luke's version, at one sentence, is the most detailed: "And as they led [Jesus] away [to be crucified], they seized one Simon of Cyrene, who was coming in from the country, and laid on him the cross, to carry it behind Jesus" (23:26). That's it. Just nineteen words in the original Greek text. An inauspicious place, you might think, to begin a reconsideration of friendship. And yet I began to think, at my friend's prompting, there's an intriguing feature of the story that may point us in a fruitful direction.

Earlier in Luke's Gospel Jesus had told the crowds, "If anyone would come after me, let him deny himself and take up his cross daily and follow me" (9:23). And later, long after the events recorded in the Gospel, the apostle Paul had written, "Bear one another's burdens, and so fulfill the law of Christ" (Gal. 6:2). Poised, as it were, between these two texts, we find Simon of Cyrene, bearing Jesus's burden as his companion on the road to

Calvary, in accord with Paul's words. Yet Simon doesn't take up his burden voluntarily, as Jesus had encouraged his followers to do. Rather, Jesus's burden has been *placed*, unexpectedly, on him. He was "seized," the Gospel says. Simon, in effect, finds himself to have become Jesus's friend. The categories of "preference" and "freedom" aren't immediately relevant here—he is, after all, marching under the glint of Roman spears—and so the only question Simon has to ask himself is what sort of friend he'll be to the one he's already, inevitably, inextricably in relationship to. If my art historian friend is right that Simon bearing Jesus's cross may be read as an icon of friendship, this feature of the text—Simon's obligation, his inescapable commitment to being, at least for a moment, Jesus's friend—might be a window into a new way of conceiving of our friendships. Taking our cues from this art, we might begin to imagine ourselves as indissolubly linked to one another, bound by the beams of Christ's cross as we walk the same road together. And we might see our task as one of strengthening the friendships in which we're already enmeshed, already walking along in. But if we do, how might our friendships begin to look different than they do now?

℃

A brief explanation of what to expect in the pages to come is in order. This book is divided into two parts, one that focuses more on the cultural background, history, and theology of friendship and another that focuses more on the actual living out of friendship. In the first chapter, I will describe why I think friendship is a relatively weak bond in many Western cultures today, why it's a form of love that's in danger of being downgraded or dismissed in our imaginations. I'll also describe why it may be a particularly sought-after form of love for certain ones among us, like me, who know ourselves to be gay and Christian.

In the second chapter, I'll be arguing that friendship can and should be understood along the lines of a vowed or committed relationship, much like a marriage or a kinship bond. Here I'll narrate some of the cultural history of friendship, telling the story of how we got to the place the first chapter describes and how we may, in our churches, be able to move into better, healthier places and practices.

The third chapter will take a step back and ask about the scriptural and theological underpinnings for our practice of friendship. If specifically Christian friendship represents a modification or transformation of earlier, pagan practices of friendship, what does that transformation consist in? What is it about the appearance of Jesus, and his death and resurrection, that changes friendship? Those are the questions I'll be trying to answer in that chapter.

Then comes part 2, which is less theoretical and more oriented toward practical questions. The fourth chapter will explore the intersection between erotic love and friendship, and I'll be suggesting, more specifically, that friendship is a form of love that many celibate people may be uniquely called to pursue. This is an urgent question, of course, for those of us who are gay and celibate, because our friendships will likely, at some time or another, face the issue of erotic attraction. But I also think it's relevant for people in opposite-sex friendships, which is a form of love that many in the church have cast a suspicious eye toward.

Chapter 5 will ask what it means to cultivate committed, promise-based friendships when most of us know all too well the disappointments and heartaches that our actual friendships can undergo. In this chapter I will try to tell, with as much honesty as I can muster, my story of losing an especially valuable friendship and how I've found hope on the other side of that loss.

And in the final chapter, I will try to lay out some concrete ways we might begin to pursue and nurture friendships in the church today. I'll offer a few specific suggestions, but I hope this chapter reads less like a blueprint and more like a provocation.

There are many—perhaps endless—ways we Christians could seek to nourish and deepen our friendships, and if this chapter prompts some more imaginative thinking along those lines, I will consider it a success.

Friendship is a good and godly love in its own right, just as worthy of attention, nurture, and respect as any other form of Christian affection. That's what the Christian tradition has mainly said. And that's what I want to say—from a fresh angle of vision—in this book, too.

PART 1

READING FRIENDSHIP

1

An Eclipse of Friendship?

If we ask ourselves whether there are a significant number
of people today without true friends, or whether our modern society is one in which friendship plays a diminishing
role, I think the answers are yes.

—Digby Anderson

But love is lost; the way of friendship's gone,
Though David had his Jonathan, Christ his John.

—George Herbert

On the eve of my confirmation, I sat in a circle in my priest's living room with the other confirmands and tried to quiet my thoughts. Dinner was finished, our dirty plates and empty wineglasses no longer balanced on our laps but set aside somewhere around the feet of our chairs. We had each finished telling our stories of coming to faith and making the decision to seek confirmation in the Church of England. Now, at the end of our evening together, our priest suggested we close with a few moments of reflection and prayer. "I'm going to come around and anoint each of you with oil," she explained. "And as I do so, I'd like you to choose one word and say it aloud, and then I'll pray for you. Pick a word that represents what you need from God as you go on in your life as a Christian. Pick a word that summarizes what you're asking of God for your future."

My inner twitch at anything that smells like Christian kitsch was set in motion at this suggestion, but I hurriedly stifled it. Hadn't I just read something about how salutary it is to humble yourself to sing the fifth-rate hymns that most Christians seem to love? I resolved to be my best nonjudgmental self that evening. Besides, I loved this priest, and if she said it, it must be worth doing.

I started thinking of what word I might choose: *Forgiveness.* I knew I would need that on an hourly basis. *Grace.* Wasn't this *the* Christian word I ought to select, if I could beat the other confirmands to it? *Mercy. Hope. Perseverance.* All good choices. The problem was that, peeking after closing my eyes and bowing my head, I could see that the priest was starting on the other side of the room, which meant that I would be the next to last person she'd come to. Which, in turn, meant that all the good words would be taken already, and I didn't want to be unoriginal. Maybe I could choose *humility* or *endurance* or *providence*—those words were just obscure enough that I doubted anyone else had thought of them.

I squeezed my eyes shut again. In a few months, I'd be moving back to the States after finishing graduate school. I'd be saying good-bye to this priest, whom I'd slowly come to love, who was now placing her hands, with their long pianist's fingers, on the head of one of my fellow confirmands. I'd be bidding farewell to dinners like this; no more curries followed by sticky toffee pudding and milky tea made by these people with funny northern accents who had first seemed like strangers and had gradually become the people I most wanted to spend my evenings with. I'd be moving to a new city where I had only acquaintances, not relatives or close friends. I had no idea where I'd go to church.

I could hear the creak of the floor as the priest stepped in front of me. I cupped my hands and looked up to see her dipping her finger in the oil. She made the sign of the cross on my palms. The scent of the rose-infused oil was suddenly overpowering and not altogether pleasant. I watched the shiny liquid pool in my hands and seep through my fingers. I hoped it wouldn't drip on my shoes.

"What word would you like me to pray for you, Wesley?" the priest whispered, her lower lip protruding and puckering in the way it always did when she tried to suppress a smile. I knew she was fond of me, and I liked the protective, mothering way she placed her hand on my head, the way her eyes were kind and gentle.

After a moment's hesitation, I said, "Friendship." And immediately I wished I could reel it back in. Hanging there in the air, waiting for her prayer, it didn't seem like a very spiritual word. It struck me suddenly as somewhat selfish, myopic, disconnected from Jesus and grace and faith, all the things this evening was supposed to be about.

But my priest knew it was what I'd been thinking about ever since I decided to take a job in Pittsburgh. Over coffee the week before, I'd told her that I was afraid of leaving the comfort of my circle of friends in England. I'd told her that I was scared I wouldn't be able to make new friends like the especially close ones I'd made in graduate school and at my church, which I loved. I found myself riffing on that final, poignant line of the movie *Stand by Me*: "I'll never have any friends later on like the ones I have right now in England. Can anyone?" Saying good-bye to friends is painful. We don't like it when, as the movie puts it, they whirl in and out of our lives like busboys.

That night, crouched in prayer in that dimly lit living room, hands upturned in a posture of receptivity, I said, wordlessly, that I needed friends for the road ahead. While the priest prayed over me, I thought, *"Friendship" was probably a good word to choose, after all. Without people to love and be loved by, I don't imagine faith is very sustainable.*

&

There's a reason I found myself praying for friendship that night in England, rather than just unreflectively counting on it to be there for me, and I think it's because I sensed its tenuous place, its ambiguous status, in our culture. A penumbra of questions and anxieties, it seems, lingers around the concept of friendship, perhaps especially for many of us navigating our late-modern world as Christians. We might be able to muster a definition and explanation of friendship's importance if we were quizzed on it, but for many of us that doesn't solve the deeper matter of why we want it so much, and why it so often seems unreachable or fraught, burdened in our own era in a way many of us imagine it wasn't in previous centuries.

Benjamin Myers, an Australian theologian, has outlined a series of ways that friendship has been eclipsed or pushed to the margins of contemporary life. He suggests that friendship in modern Western societies has been obscured by various myths, to the point that we can't see our way clear anymore to understand friendship the way we once did and embrace it along with its ancient practitioners. Myers traces the first of these myths back to Sigmund Freud's suspicion that all relationships, at base, involve eroticism—that the desire for sex is the secret truth of every relationship, so that any mutual liking or interest must be something *more* than chaste affection. And many cultural observers nowadays would apparently concur, as we will see in the pages below.

For instance, notice how some of us wonder about—and make light of or poke fun at or even feel embarrassed or ashamed of—the perception of romantic longing seeping into our same-sex friendships. In pursuing this line of thought, especially in its stronger forms where we treat any close male friendship as just inevitably homosexual, we are treating sex as a *myth* in the traditional meaning of the word—a story we tell ourselves that seems to illumine the hitherto misunderstood hinterland of a thing. With male friendship, where certain previous eras might have seen two people who merely admired each other and wanted to spur each other on to greater heights of maturity and virtue, in the modern West we're more attuned to the possibility of an underlying, subconscious erotic attraction.[1] And that mythology contributes to the anxiety or humorous uncertainty many of us feel about friendship today.

In the time of the Second World War, well before the so-called sexual revolution, C. S. Lewis was already defending the nonsexual character of friendship against critics who thought that any time two men were close, their camaraderie was "really homosexual." Such a verdict, Lewis points out, is akin to the claim that there's an invisible cat in the chair: if you question the assertion, the very lack of evidence may be marshaled as proof ("If there were an invisible cat in that chair, the chair would look empty; but the chair does look empty; therefore there is an invisible cat in it").

More recently, moviegoers have been noting the spate of Hollywood "bromantic" comedies—movies that focus on two guys getting to know each other, navigating the ups and downs of learning how to be friends, but *not* hopping into bed together.

1. Consider this comment from the British writer A. C. Grayling, exemplifying the kind of suspicion I'm talking about: "Of the famous friendships recorded in history and legend, most are between men and most of these in turn appear not to be friendships as such but homosexual loves, which raises the question whether much of the thinking about friendship in classical antiquity and afterwards is about a very special and intense version of it, focused upon erotic attraction and its fulfillments." There's little concrete evidence to support Grayling's perspective here, but he manages effectively to conjure a cloud of suspicion anyway.

Films like *Superbad* and *I Love You, Man*, to choose only two
of the recent array, show us the awkwardness of two men trying
to achieve some kind of emotional closeness—to *love* each other,
without saying the word—and at the same time avoid getting
labeled as a couple. A tough gig, apparently. You can hear a
bit of defensive, self-deprecating humor in actor Seth Rogen's
voice as he tries to explain why the same all-male crew makes
an appearance in each new Judd Apatow flick: "We're all really
uncomfortable around girls, for the most part. I imagine that has
something to do with it." This myth—that sex must be there,
humming along like an engine that powers the relationship, even
if the friends themselves aren't always aware of it—is something
many of us are starting to joke about. It's a trope that's entering
our common stock of cultural observations.

Not long ago, I read a novel by William Maxwell that brought
this quandary to mind again for me. Written in 1945, *The Folded
Leaf* tells the story of two boys, Spud and Lymie, who befriend
each other while they're both still in their teens and then deepen
their friendship as students at the same university. After starting
college, they join the same fraternity and share a room. Among
the many tender passages in this exquisitely told story, here's
one that describes a typical night for the two young men:

> [Spud] and Lymie were always the first ones to go up to the
> dorm. In the big icy-cold bed they clung to each other, shivering
> like puppies, until the heat of their bodies began to penetrate
> through the outing flannel of their pajamas and their heavy
> woolen bathrobes. Lymie slept on his right side and Spud curled
> against him, with his fists in the hollow of Lymie's back. In five
> minutes the whole bed was warmed and Spud was sound asleep.
> It took Lymie longer, as a rule. He lay there, relaxed and drowsy,
> aware of the cold outside the covers, and of the warmth com-
> ing to him from Spud, and Spud's odor, which was not stale or
> sweaty or like the odor of any other person. Then he moved his
> right foot until the outer part of the instep came in contact with

Spud's bare toes, and from this one point of reality he swung out safely into darkness, into no sharing whatever.

Scanning the internet for readers' reactions to this novel, I found critics who felt certain that Spud and Lymie's relationship was a homosexual one. In 1945, these readers noted, this elliptical description of a shared bed was the only way Maxwell had available to him to indicate the erotic nature of his characters' love for each other. Had he been more overt, he might have faced censorship. Perhaps these critics are right, but I can't banish Lewis's metaphor from my imagination—in the case of an invisible cat, any lack of cat sightings can be read as confirmation of the cat's existence. And besides, this passage is all Maxwell gives us. We can fill in the picture ourselves, creating a sexual encounter from these raw materials. But it will be only that—our creation—and the novel as it stands could just as easily be read as a testimony to a kind of relationship we've apparently forgotten, or perhaps disbelieve, ever existed: a nonsexual, physically intimate same-sex friendship.

It's not just movies and novels that highlight this Freudian mythology of sex, though. Evidence from the social sciences, too, points to the prevalence of this particular myth. Niobe Way, a sociologist at New York University, has recently published the results of several years of her research into the development of adolescent male friendships, and her findings dovetail with what Seth Rogen joked about. Way's book, *Deep Secrets: Boys' Friendships and the Crisis of Connection*, describes a recurring pattern. When they're in their early teens, the boys she interviewed often talked about their same-sex friendships in surprisingly intimate terms. Most of the boys described their best friend as someone with whom they could let their guard down, unburden their deepest secrets (hence the title of Way's book), and find a level of mutual commitment. But Way found that as these boys grew older, by the time they

arrived in their late teens, many of them were no longer willing
to speak in such shockingly intimate terms about their friends.
Prefacing their remarks with "no homo," they would articulate
the place of friendship in their lives differently than they had
only a few years before.[2] One of Way's conclusions is that, as
they mature, these boys find no cultural space for the friendships they once enjoyed. Fearing they might be suspected of
being gay, they retreat from same-sex intimacy. They don't give
up gay sex, since that was never a part of these relationships
to begin with, but they do surrender the close camaraderie
they once felt.[3]

This myth, then—the belief that sex wholly explains the
depths of our most profound relationships—has led many of
us in recent decades to feel suspicious of, uncertain about, and
at times even ashamed of deep friendships ("If I get too close
to him, will people think we're attracted to each other? *Are*
we attracted to each other?") and has hindered our search for
closer and more fulfilling ones. As my friend John says, we men
are quick to give the three slaps on the back of the friend we're
hugging, each one of which stands for a single word: "I'm. Not.
Gay." And after giving that hug, we try hard to preserve some

2. It's also worth noting that there are certain trends that cut against the grain
of the ones Way describes. Eric Anderson at the University of Bath "found that 89
per cent of white undergraduate men at two UK universities and one sixth from
college, said they were happy to kiss another man on the lips through friendship." What cultural and contextual differences may account for this difference,
I'm not sure.

3. A reader comments: "When the Sudanese 'Lost Boys' first arrived in
the US, they would frequently hold hands with each other as a sign of their
friendship. We observed this many times after church. Gradually, they began
to hear that here this would be understood as implying a sexual relationship,
and they were incredulous. There was a news show with Tom Brokaw that
profiled some of these guys. One of them asked Tom Brokaw whether this
was true, and Brokaw conceded, haltingly, that here it would indeed be seen
as representing something sexual. The look in the Lost Boys' faces was one of
intense and painful dismay. We noticed with our Sudanese foster son and his
cohort that, except in extremely private contexts, the practice stopped almost
instantly."

kind of closeness but, at the same time, keep it moderated with an appropriate distance.

৪০

But concern about sex isn't the only potential threat to friendship. There's another myth that endangers our appreciation and cultivation of friendship, and that's what we might call the myth of the ultimate significance of marriage and the nuclear family. Many of us believe that there can be no closer bonds than those between siblings, spouses, and children and that friendship must, of necessity, take a backseat to blood ties. Considering contemporary Western secular and religious communities, one is tempted to say that friendship's number one enemy, at least over the past half century or so, is the elevated importance we have attached to spousal, parental, and extended familial bonds.

A recent dinner out with my sister brought this point home to me. With my younger brother about to get engaged, we started speculating about whom he might ask to be his best man. "Tyler?" I offered in between bites of corn chips and salsa, tossing out the name of one of his closest friends in Denver, where he lives. "No way!" my sister replied. "He'll ask *you*." She continued, "When it comes down to it, Tyler could move away and be out of his life in a year. But you're his *brother*. You're *family*. That's the closest bond he'll ever have." Perhaps she's right, but the fact that she couldn't imagine things being otherwise shows the uncertain place friendship occupies in our culture when we compare it to family connections.

Several years ago, a writer named Carrie English wrote a disarming essay in the *Boston Globe* titled "A Bridesmaid's Lament." Not only was she mourning the loss of one particular friendship—her friend was getting married and thus, in a sense, leaving English behind—but she was also lamenting the absence of any acceptable way in our culture to *express* that sense of loss that her friend's wedding brought with it. In her words,

In the vows they wrote, the bride and groom gushed about how lucky they were to have found someone who loved them unconditionally—someone who made anyplace home—someone who was their best friend. And I stood there under the flower-covered gazebo thinking: "Why not me?" . . . I was thinking: "She loves *me* unconditionally. The house *we* shared always felt like home. And I thought *we* were best friends."

Surely I can't be the only person who feels like weddings are a bit of a rejection—two people announcing in public that they love each other more than they love you. . . . There's no denying that weddings change friendships forever. Priorities have been declared in public. She'll be there for him in sickness and in health, till death do they part. She'll be there for *you* on your birthday or when he has to work late.

Being platonically dumped wouldn't be so bad if people would acknowledge you have the right to be platonically heartbroken. But it's just not part of our vocabulary. However much our society might pay lip service to friendship, the fact remains that the only love it considers important—important enough to merit a huge public celebration—is romantic love.

English concludes her essay by recommending something truly revolutionary, something we'll return to in the pages below: make promises to be there for your friends.

I urge you all to go out, buy some champagne, bake a cake, and throw a fancy anniversary party for your friends. Have your guests toast to a lifetime of *Bridget Jones* marathons and road trips to Wrentham. And renew your vows to be there for one another through thick and thin—even after all of you are married.

English's lament makes the same point my sister was making, only from a different angle. Where my sister was celebrating the way family often trumps friendship, English was ruing friendship's displacement. Both agree, though, in their observation that friendship often finds itself in danger of being eclipsed by the brightness of our commitment to our nuclear families.

And once the wedding day is over and kids come along, many friendships may disappear altogether. This may be something both the married couple themselves, as well as their friends (married or single), regret, but it is still often treated as an irreversible fact of life. We may wish things could go on as before, but in our moments of realism, we know they can't. If it comes to making time to be with friends or returning home to preserve marital or parental intimacy, the choice is clear: the sacrifices friendship warrants have their limits, and they dare not cut too deeply into quality time spent with family members. This mythology of family threatens to demote friendship from an honored place in our culture, and we're often left feeling anxious or unsure about how to shore up our friendships in the face of it.

༄

Returning to Myers's list of mythologies that obscure our view of friendship, there are others, too. Reductive evolutionary biology and psychology, in which all human loves must be understood in terms of hardwired self-interest, have little place for friendship. "In [the evolutionary] worldview, the meaning of every human activity lies in its origin," he suggests. "Everything is traced back to some basic instinct, some survival function. It's easy to view marriage, family, politics, and work along these lines—but friendship disappears, since it's not a natural bond." There's also the related myth of work and output: we *are*—we have an identity—only insofar as we find a vocation that contributes something to society. But this viewpoint diminishes that "activity" which has no other goal in view than the mutual enjoyment and appreciation of each other: friendship. "Where our relationships are defined in terms of work, usefulness, and productivity," Myers concludes, "friendship disappears."

But I'd like to add one more myth to Myers's list, one that's implicit in what he says yet isn't stated overtly. It's the myth of what we might term, simply, *freedom*—the myth that the less encumbered and entangled I am, or the less accountable and anchored I am to a particular relationship, the better able I am to find my truest self and secure real happiness. This myth is so ingrained in our imaginations, I suspect, that it may undergird and nurture all the other myths Myers mentions. And it's not hard to see how it strikes at the root of friendship. If your deepest fulfillment is found in personal autonomy, then friendship—or at least the close kind I want to recommend in these pages—is more of a liability than an asset.

Single people, perhaps, perceive especially keenly the consequences of this myth of freedom. One of the characters in Willa Cather's novel *Shadows on the Rock* says, "Only solitary men know the full joys of friendship. Others have their family; but to a solitary and an exile his friends are everything." By the same token, I'd say that only solitary people know the full sorrows of friendship's gradual diminishment in our culture as we maintain our commitment to maximal individual autonomy. I talk regularly with many of these people: men and women who have passed the usual age for marriage and child rearing and who turn to the church, hoping to find a robust vision of committed friendship, only to encounter a looser, more casual form of social life that seems to say, *We can be friends, so long as it doesn't require too many sacrifices.*

But it's not just single people who are harmed by our commitment to the myth of freedom. Married couples and parents stand to lose as well. Over the last several months, I've had poignant conversations with several friends who are young mothers. They all tell me the same story. When you're at home caring for an infant or a toddler, it can be easy to feel as though your world is contracting, and you're left scrabbling your way along a lightless tunnel by yourself, your only companion a drooling, jabbering creature who can't sympathize with your needs and engage you in meaningful conversation. Your friends have stopped inviting you out to eat because they assume you're putting the baby to bed at just the time the main course is being ordered. You're not able to go out for lunch or an afternoon shopping excursion because that's when your toddler's nap time starts. One of these mothers informed me that there's even a lively discussion in the "mommy blogosphere" about young mother-friend pickup lines: "I see we have the same stroller—would you ever want to get together for a walk in the park?" And suddenly, not unlike Carrie English's description of being single at your best friend's wedding, you start to feel like your friends *are* everything to you, that they're all you want—but also that you don't know how to hang onto them, or even if you can make friends to begin with.

I've talked with yet others—retirees, divorced people, the newly married—who have found that marriage does *not* meet all one's relational needs. They're all aware of their need for deeper friendships, and not just romantic or spousal love, which puts them in good company historically but, sadly, out of step with much of the rhetoric they hear at church marriage retreats and on Christian radio programs. Stephanie Coontz has shown how unusual, compared to past cultures, our contemporary scene is when it invests marriage with more significance than it can reasonably hold:

> Through most of history, it was considered dangerously anti-social to be too emotionally attached to one's spouse, because that diluted loyalties to family, neighbours, and society at large. Until the mid-19th-century, the word "love" was used more frequently to describe feelings for neighbours, relatives and fellow church members than spouses.
>
> The emotional lives of Victorian middle-class women revolved around passionate female bonds that overshadowed the "respectful affection" they felt for their husbands. Men, too,

sought intimacy outside the family circle. A man could write a
letter to his betrothed recounting his pleasure at falling asleep
on the bosom of his best friend without fearing that she might
think him gay. When couples first began to go on honeymoons
in the 19th century they often took family and friends along
for company.[4]

All that is, of course, largely lost now, and the result is that even
many people who know the highs and lows of marital bliss, and
thus might be thought not to need friendship like single people
do, are freshly aware of what the eclipse of friendship means for
them, too. After buying into the myth that "(romantic/family)
love is all you need," and that one is happiest when least tied
down, as the myth of freedom promises, they've come to see
these things as just that—myths—and ones that leave them still
hungry for the quieter, less advertised love of friendship.

୫

My own story of feeling the loss of friendship has something
to do with my marital state and, along with that, my sexuality. As I've written about elsewhere, I find myself caught in
a place of tension between my Christian faith and my sexual
orientation that makes me particularly eager to cultivate close
friendships but also especially fearful of not being able to find
and sustain them.

It was in late high school that I finally admitted to myself what
I must have known for a decade or more: that I was romantically

---

4. On this point, compare Craig A. Williams's discussion of classical Roman
ideals: "Marriage was not traditionally described as the unique locus of a special type of love between two individuals: that was the function of, precisely,
friendship. Indeed, there is a noticeable tendency throughout the Latin textual
tradition to idealize friendship more highly than marriage, and in doing so to
use imagery familiar from later celebrations of romantic love and marriage. The
motif of the friend as *alter ego*, for example, corresponds to modern idealizing of
one's spouse or partner as 'my other half' (or the even more self-effacing 'better
half'), yet nowhere in surviving ancient texts is it applied to husbands and wives."

drawn—mysteriously, powerfully, and almost exclusively—to other guys, not girls. Even in elementary school, the friends I developed crushes on were boys. And in my last couple of years of high school, I finally accepted that the usual terms— "homosexual," "gay," "queer," and their equivalents—were terms that described me, even though my experience of gay community and culture was virtually nonexistent. I'd never had a boyfriend or visited a place like Boystown. All I knew was that what I was feeling for the guys my age didn't seem to be a mere passing fascination that would sort itself out once I weathered the storm of puberty. It seemed, instead, to settle into a deep-seated desire for intimacy that became as much a part of my basic makeup as my height or right-handedness. At times, it seemed to verge on the religious or transcendent, which, I surmised, is how many people feel about romantic attraction, no matter its objects. Desire led me out of myself and left me transfixed, trembling with wonder at the faces, bodies, and personalities of the guys my age whom I began to notice around me. Sure, I wanted the usual friend stuff that many high school boys want—a gang to go hiking and camping with, people to join me at the movies, comrades for games and parties (we played a lot of bumper pool in high school, my friends and I), the chance to goof off with a few people who know and like you for who you are. But I also wanted something more. In my most secret fantasies, I wanted a physical, emotional, even *spiritual* closeness—a reciprocally exclusive affection—that I couldn't quite bring myself to describe, even in the privacy of my own reveries.

At the same time, I was becoming more aware of my Christian faith and its importance to me. I had been raised in the church, a Southern Baptist, and baptized as a boy. Now, though, in the firestorm of puberty (of all times), I wanted to *own* my Christian identity, to get to know it and claim it consciously for myself. I remember, for instance, reading about what I now know to be the tradition of contemplative prayer, with its goal of turning each moment of the day into a kind of God-filled sanctuary, and I said to my youth pastor, with all the idealism of my young age in tow, "That's what I want to do—learn how to pray continuously." It wasn't, for me, a matter of whether to be gay *or* Christian; I knew that I was *both*, somehow, and that eventually, not then, I'd have to figure out how to square that circle.

But as I grew older, I realized what I hadn't been fully aware of when I was pondering these things in my high school years: there were churches I could join that would affirm, encourage, and support me if I wanted to try to find a husband. Looking back on it now, I could have easily decided that one of those churches was the solution to my turmoil. What became increasingly troubling, though, was that this affirmation of same-sex marriage was not the position of the church throughout the ages, nor was it a position embraced by the churches I had been a part of and wanted to remain a part of. If I decided I wanted to find a partner, I'd have to swim against the current of what faithful Christians, with almost total unanimity, had understood Scripture to be saying about our creation as male and female and the meaning of Christian marriage.

"It is with [God's] Yes to the [person] elected and loved and called by Him that He says No to his sinful existence," writes Karl Barth, and I heard both—"Yes" and "No"—as I started to pay attention to what historic, orthodox Christian teaching had to say about our sexual lives. There is a divine "Yes" to marriage and sexual intimacy between a man and a woman, premised on their bodily difference that seemed to gesture toward (albeit faintly) the transcendent difference of Creator from creature. But that "Yes" also seemed to disclose a corresponding "No" to sexual intimacy in any other context. God created humanity male and female, as the book of Genesis describes (1:27; 2:18–25), and when Jesus appeared on the scene, after humanity's fall, he set about healing and restoring God's originally beautiful creation rather than replacing it with something entirely new. Jesus hallowed what had previously existed between Adam and Eve. "A man shall leave his father and his mother and hold fast to his wife, and the two shall become one flesh," he told his disciples (Matt. 19:5). This, it seemed, was God's "Yes" to sex, to marriage, the divine endorsement of erotic love. And throughout Scripture, that "Yes" appeared to entail a "No" to any sexual relationship that might deviate from it. Christ died and rose from death for the *redemption*, not the setting aside, of our gendered bodies, and it's on that basis that the gospel says "No" to same-sex sexual relationships.

This focus on gender difference—rather than, as some revisionist interpretations have it, the alleged presence of "exploitation" or an "excess of desire" in homosexual unions—went a long way toward explaining Paul's denunciation of same-sex erotic behavior in his letter to the Romans (see 1:26–27). In their immediate context, Paul's descriptions of homosexuality link it to humanity's turn away from the Creator to images of their fellow creatures. Difference is exchanged for sameness. Paul is up in arms not about pedophilia or temple prostitution, it seems, but rather about how the original creation of male and female has been set aside. Humanity turns away from God and worships images of itself (1:25), and sexual relationships, correspondingly, exchange engagement with the other (men with women, women with men) for engagement with the same. The communion of God with his creation, which was mirrored in man's turning toward woman and vice versa, breaks down in homosexual relationships, and thus the meaning of marriage and gender difference is obscured. Reading Scripture this way, I eventually decided that I couldn't in good conscience join an "affirming" church and hope to find a husband.

What I feared most, though, about my decision to remain celibate was that I had thereby doomed myself to lifelong loneliness. When I was still in high school, despite being gay, I often daydreamed about what it would be like to be married, to have a house and children, to have a home of the sort I had growing up, to know that I belonged somewhere. Now, in light of where I felt my Christian faith was taking me, I stopped dreaming about those things. In their place, I began to have a recurrent picture of myself around age sixty, coming home to an empty apartment, having lived all of my adulthood as a single man. I started to think about the particulars of that scenario: not knowing each year where I'd be for Christmas, waking up each morning to a quiet bedroom and having no one across the table from me as I ate my cereal before heading to work, coming home at the end of the day and reading a book with no one to talk to about the parts of it that stood out to me. I began to resonate with what Lauren Winner has called "the loneliness of the everyday": "the loneliness of no one knowing if your plane lands on time, of no one to call if you lock yourself out of your house or your alternator dies—I find that loneliness worse [than the loneliness that comes as a result of a breakup or a divorce]."

And I began to wonder what, if anything, to do about it.

☙

My primary question, over time, became a question about love. Where was I to find love? Where was I to *give* love? If Scripture and the Christian tradition were right that I shouldn't try to find a husband, surely the apparent corollary couldn't also be right—that I was therefore cut off from any deep, meaningful form of intimacy and communion. Could it?

In P. T. Anderson's masterpiece, *Magnolia*, one of the characters—the decidedly hard-to-like "quiz kid" Donnie Smith— bursts out, "I don't know where to put things, you know? I really do have love to give! I just don't know where to put it!" Well into middle age, Donnie has just gotten braces. There's a bartender—handsome, lithe, tanned; in his twenties, probably— whom Donnie has fallen for, and he wants to impress him with the sheen of a good smile. Soon enough, however, it becomes clear that the bartender isn't interested in a relationship with Donnie. And that's when Donnie blurts out that he does have love to give—the problem is how to channel it, how to find the right relationship in which it can flourish, how to find its place. I know exactly what he means.

And I've come to think that the best response to Donnie's cry may be from another drama, Tom Stoppard's *The Invention of Love*, a play about the life of the poet and classicist A. E. Housman. Toward the middle of the play, there's a scene in which Housman, twentysomething at the time, meets his departed self, his older mirror image who now inhabits the underworld. The two Housmans—the younger known as "Housman," the older by his initials "AEH"—have an extended conversation in which they discuss, among other things, the ancient Greco-Roman ideal of friendship, *amicitia*. Bygone ages knew of the heroic possibility of being "comrades in arms," in which the love of men for other men could be channeled into self-sacrifice on the battlefield—the Sacred Band of Theban youths, for example, who died in pairs at the battle of Chaeronea. Hearing his older self recount the tale, the younger Housman, himself a homosexual, avows, "I would be such a friend to someone."

To this day, years after reading Stoppard's play at the recommendation of a friend who told me it had changed his view of homosexuality, I find that that line gives voice to my desire, too: *I would be such a friend to someone.* More than that, I'm inspired by Housman's conviction that there was an established historical ideal and practice—friendship or comradeship as a recognized, respected institution—that speaks, down through centuries long past, to his present need. Housman is convinced he's found the answer to Donnie's lament. There *is*, in fact, a place for love, and it's called friendship.

As someone trying to reconcile his Christian faith with his homosexuality, I have become increasingly drawn to that notion:

that there exists, for someone like me, a location for my love. That, by rediscovering ancient, and not-so-ancient, forms and exemplars of friendship, I might be able to rewrite the lonely future I feared would be my lot as a celibate gay Christian. That I too am called to nurture, deepen, and sanctify my love.

And that's how I found myself praying for friendship that night in my priest's living room. Now, I'm praying for it not just for myself but also for others—single, married, gay, straight, and otherwise—in the church today. I'm convinced that all of us could benefit from a recovery of friendship as a genuine love in its own right. We've largely forgotten it, but I'm praying we can find it again.

2

"I Love You Because You're Mine"

Friendship is voluntary, unlike kinship; it retains its voluntary character, unlike marriage.

—Diogenes Allen

Friendship should be like a marriage: for better for worse, for richer for poorer, till death depart. They cannot be separated whom true amity knitteth.

—Richard Morison to Thomas Cromwell, 1538

In December 1943, several months after he had been imprisoned by the Nazis, the Lutheran theologian and pastor Dietrich Bonhoeffer wrote to his newly married friend Eberhard Bethge: "When you characterize marriage as what 'remains stable in all passing relationships,' you are certainly right. But don't we also count a good friendship among the things that remain stable?" You can almost hear Dietrich—I'll call him by

his first name, since I'm describing his correspondence with
his friends and family members—voicing a bit of insecurity,
wondering about his own status as Eberhard's comrade, much
like the bridesmaid Carrie English I mentioned in the previous
chapter.

Eberhard wrote back:

> You write that, apart from marriage, our friendship should
> count as one of the things that remain stable. But just this is
> not so in the estimation of others and the consideration they
> give it. It is marriage—whether it is the more stable of the two
> or not—that gets the outward consideration and recognition.
> Everyone, in this case the whole family, must take it into ac-
> count and thinks it right that much has to be done, and should
> be done, on behalf of a married couple. Friendship, even when
> it's so exclusive and includes all of each other's goods, as it is
> with us, doesn't have any *"necessitas,"* as Father expressed it
> in regard to applying for a permit to visit [you in prison]. It's
> taken for granted that your letters are passed to Maria [your
> fiancée], and almost as much that they will go to Karl-Friedrich
> [your older brother], but it takes an extra struggle for me to
> get them as well.

In other words, Eberhard wants to grant Dietrich's point that
friendship is a stable, permanent good alongside marriage, but
he's too much of a realist not to point out the problems with
that viewpoint. The prison guards won't even give Eberhard
permission to visit Dietrich, and Dietrich's older brother, with
whom Dietrich isn't as close as he is with Eberhard, receives
Dietrich's letters before Eberhard does. In the light of those
unyielding circumstances, can it be said, when it really counts,
that Eberhard's and Dietrich's relationship is as fixed and anchored as Eberhard's relationship with his spouse is? Is it true
that friendship is as secure and easily recognizable as a public,
vowed, perduring bond like marriage?

Eberhard's letter prompted a further response from Dietrich. In January 1944, he wrote back—somewhat cryptically—that friendship, "unlike marriage and family relationships, . . . doesn't enjoy any generally recognized rights but depends entirely on its own inherent quality." And this, in turn, leads him into an interesting discussion of what that mysterious "inherent quality" might consist in. What sphere of life, Dietrich asks—the sphere of duty? of religion and spirituality? or some other realm?—should we place friendship in? What kind of love is friendship? Whatever answer we settle on, he concludes, friendship can't belong to the realm of obligation. "I believe that, within this realm of freedom, friendship is by far the rarest . . . and the most precious good," he rhapsodizes, sounding somewhat wistful. But he doesn't actually address the concern Eberhard had raised. If friendship doesn't have some kind of public recognition of the sort Eberhard enjoyed with his wife, then what, really, *were* Eberhard and Dietrich to each other, and how might their love be preserved and sustained? It's all well and good to sing friendship's praises, but too often that's like waxing eloquent about a field of daylilies: you can enjoy them while they last, but don't count on them being there the next morning.

Years after this exchange of letters, after Dietrich had been executed in a Nazi prison camp, Eberhard fielded a question from a member of an audience who had gathered to hear him speak about his old friend. Surely, the questioner said, "it must [have been] a homosexual partnership" that existed between Eberhard and Dietrich—after all, what else could Dietrich's impassioned letters have signaled?

Notice how we have here, in the prison letters and in Eberhard's speaking engagement, two different responses to the problem of friendship. First, there's Eberhard's and Dietrich's dawning awareness that their friendship was fragile, potentially unrecognized by the people who matter most (whether that be fellow family members or Nazi prison guards). And second, there's a later audience member's curiosity and incredulity about the nature of the two men's relationship—surely they must have been gay. Taken together, these two reactions nicely illustrate a particular feeling about friendship that has, arguably, grown more pronounced in the years since Dietrich and Eberhard wrote to each other. That feeling is perhaps best described with words like *suspicion, unsettledness,* or *doubt.* I, at least, have become uncertain about what I can count on friendship to be. I want it to be something solid and substantial, but I'm sober enough to realize there are forces working against my considering it that way.

Others, I suspect, share my questions about the possibility of intimacy between two friends, particularly when those friends are of the same sex. Like Eberhard and Dietrich, we may wonder about friendship's lack of official, public identification. Does that mean it's a weaker, less reliable bond than marriage or family ties? And like Eberhard's interlocutor, many of us entertain doubts about whether it's really possible to attain intimacy without others suspecting some sexual motive or complication in the relationship. Can you keep getting closer and closer to a same-sex friend, we may wonder, and not end up having the friendship classified as homosexual?

When you put all these uncertainties and misgivings together, it's easy to doubt whether friendship is robust enough, in our day and age, to nourish people like the young mothers I mentioned earlier, or the gay Christians like me who are looking for places where we can give and receive genuine love. Is Dietrich right? Is friendship best understood as a kind of "play," freed from any "necessary" public recognition and therefore a sort of optional extra—nice if you can get it, but don't hold your breath while you wait? And if it is such a weak, ephemeral thing, are we better off looking for meaningful intimacy elsewhere?

ɞ

In 1914, just after a young Dietrich Bonhoeffer had moved
to Berlin with his family amid the gathering storm clouds of
the First World War, several hundred miles to the east, an eccentric Russian polymath published a book of theology in the
form of twelve letters addressed to an anonymous friend. The
author, a young man named Pavel Florensky, had an unusual
craving for friendship. As one of his fellow students described
him, Florensky, "when he takes someone to his heart . . . puts
everything into the relationship." Not content with mere ac-
quaintanceship, Florensky

> wants to draw his friend into every detail of his life and enters
> wholeheartedly into their life and interests; he'll abandon his
> own business, his acquaintance, his pressing work, if his time
> is needed (or if it seems to him that his time is needed) by his
> friend. He and Vasia eat from one bowl and not for anything
> will he sit down to dine without him, however late he may be;
> he goes to talk to his doctor, helps him with written work, in
> general doesn't leave him time to draw breath. That is what
> true friendship should be like, but only given total reciprocity;
> otherwise it's an insupportable burden, I know that by my own
> experience.

Whatever Florensky's sexual orientation may have been—
he eventually, to the shock of many who knew him, married
a woman—we know that he cared especially about strengthening the bonds between male friends. When he was still a
young adult, he and his friend Sergei, an Orthodox priest's
son, exchanged vows of commitment, pledging fidelity to each
other even as they made promises to remain celibate. According to his biographer, Florensky regarded this pact "as binding as a marriage or monastic vow." (In the Russian Orthodox
Church of Florensky's day, this was not unprecedented: the

ancient East knew a liturgical rite that goes by the name of *adelphōpoiēsis*—"brother-making"—for just such occasions. We'll return to this point below.)

In his theological letters, *The Pillar and Ground of the Truth*, Florensky explains what he understood himself to be doing in making such a commitment. "There are many temptations to turn away from a Friend, to remain alone or to start new relationships," he wrote. "But a person who has broken off one friendship will break off another, and a third, because he has replaced the way of ascesis"—the way of costly, self-sacrificial love—"with the desire for . . . comfort." But by pledging to be there for one particular friend, come what may, Florensky thought he could better learn the real meaning of Christian love. "The greatest . . . love is realizable," he concluded, "only in relation to *friends*, not in relation to all people, not 'in general.'"

Elsewhere Florensky compared this particular love of one friend for another to a molecular bond. Just as an organism isn't ultimately about subatomic particles or even cells but rather about chemical *connections*, so too the church isn't reducible to individuals but rather to pairs of friends. We aren't called to exist as isolated units who love God in distinction from those around us. Instead, we're told, the love of God is manifested in our love—not for our spouses or children or extended family, first and foremost, but for our *friends* (John 15:13).

Only when you spend time with letters like Pavel Florensky's—and we'll meet them again in the pages to come—does it become clear how Eberhard Bethge's and Dietrich Bonhoeffer's perspectives on friendship don't have to be the last word on the subject. True, speaking of friendship as the freest of loves and the least publicly recognized does make sense in our late-modern world—a world in which old friends can be left behind as quickly as we sign a contract for a new job halfway across the country—but that hasn't always been the case. By contrast, Florensky's hope for a sealed, vowed commitment between spiritual brothers represents one of the primary ways that all the major strands of the Christian church, both East and West, used to think about friendship before the dawning of the modern world. And the story of how that vision flourished—and then was lost—is captivating and full of intrigue.

&

Rounding the bend in the road from the village of Thirsk in North Yorkshire, your first glimpse of Rievaulx Abbey will take your breath away. One minute you're on a back-country road, charmed enough by the gentle slopes and green of the farmlands, but unprepared for the soaring flash of mottled gray-and-brown stone walls and arches. The next minute you're staring at an eleventh-century Cistercian ruin, lying like a half-remembered treasure unearthed in a wooded dale. Coming from the opposite direction, from the east, you might have the reaction my friend described to me once in an email: "I've only ever approached Rievaulx on foot, after the over-the-moors-and-through-the-forest walk from Helmsley, but whenever I go there I imagine those first monks standing in that valley, with the lovely little river running through it and the low wooded hills to break the wind, and saying, 'Yes. This is the place.'"

My one visit to Rievaulx was a pilgrimage of sorts, to honor Aelred, the abbey's fourth abbot who ruled the Benedictine community from 1147 until his death in 1167. Known best for his works *On Spiritual Friendship* and *The Mirror of Charity*, in which he sketched a vision for monastic community, Aelred has become the unofficial patron saint of friendship, owing to his powerful depiction of the spiritual fruitfulness of same-sex love. I went to Rievaulx out of gratitude for that witness. I stood in what remains of the abbot's quarters—now just a stone outline indicating where the four walls would have been—and said a prayer, thankful for an author who said of friendship what we moderns tend to reserve only for marital love: "See to what

limits love should reach among friends, namely to a willingness
to die for each other."

Distinguishing between "carnal" or "worldly" friendship,
on the one hand, and a higher, Christlike friendship, on the
other, Aelred maintained, in the face of his detractors' suspi-
cions and misgivings, that two or more monks could achieve
a holy, purified intimacy that involved something like kinship
ties or spousal promises. Echoing Cicero, he wrote, "Friendship is agreement in things human and divine, with good will
and charity," but it was his christological retooling of Cicero
that sealed the argument: "Though challenged, though injured,
though tossed into the flames, though nailed to a cross, *a friend
loves always.*" The reason monks could forge such deep bonds
of friendship, Aelred thought, is that Christ had already shown
them the way. Moreover, Christ had not only permitted the love
of friendship but positively endorsed it; when he came to specify
the "greater love" than which no one can ever have, he reached
for the image of friendship: "that someone lay down his life
for his friends" (John 15:13). That, to Aelred, was the highest
possible praise. (It was the same Gospel text Pavel Florensky
was to highlight centuries later.)

Aelred's vision of friendship was bound up with his and the
other monks' vows of celibacy.[1] Too much unreflective con-

---

1. This is important to keep in mind, for both exemplary and cautionary reasons. As my friend Joshua Gonnerman has written: "As we are reading through
St. Aelred's discussion of friendship, we must always remember that it takes place
in a very specific context, namely the monastic. Vowed celibacy, commitment to
a very particular communal setting, shared life and prayer, and even (in a very
real sense) renunciation of personal identity are all in the background against
which these discussions take place. Most of us are reading it from contexts that
differ markedly from that of Aelred. We live in a secular society, and one which is
highly individualistic. As much as we may disavow secularism and individualism,
they remain a part of our lives, and we do not go so far as to renounce personal
identity and adopt a new identity found in a highly specific and geographically
localized community. Community in Catholic contexts is either ignored or an
abstract ideal more than a concrete reality; most Catholics tend to skulk around
the back of the church, and dart out as soon as the priest is no longer in sight.

temporary thinking views sexual abstinence, ongoing sexual desire, and committed love as irreconcilable, but Aelred, and the whole monastic movement he represents, disagreed. They didn't view their choice to forego intimate physical relations and pledge themselves to a community as the renunciation of intimacy. If anything, they thought the inverse: that celibacy enabled the elevation and purification of desire, rendering love *more* substantial, not less. (I think here of that moving scene from the 2010 French film *Of Gods and Men*, in which one of the monks, Brother Luc, talks to a local Algerian girl about love. She wonders aloud what it's like to be in love, implying but not stating that she's really asking for herself and her recent infatuation. When Luc replies, "Something inside you comes alive, but you're in turmoil, especially the first time," we, the viewers, realize that this is no sheltered prude speaking; Luc knows whereof he speaks. And when the girl asks Luc if *he's* ever been in love and he says, "Yes, several times," we know he's telling the truth. Then there's this: "Then I experienced an even greater love and I answered that call. Sixty years ago." *An even greater love*—that's the monastic vision in a nutshell.)

Aelred, however, went further than many of his fellow monks when he insisted that monks weren't just called to love all their brothers, indiscriminately (although that was the baseline expectation). He also made room for especially close bonds of mutual trust and affection between certain monks:

> Divine authority commands that many more be received to the clasp of charity than to the embrace of friendship. By the law of charity we are ordered to welcome into the bosom of love not only our friends but also our enemies. But we call friends

---

Sanctification of the day through the Divine Office is not a part of the life of most Catholics; for those for whom it is, it is usually not a communal celebration. . . . The recognition of these fundamental differences leads to the question: is what Aelred talks about possible for those living secular lives in the world? Is it presumption to transpose this kind of friendship from that context to our own?"

only those to whom we have no qualm about entrusting our heart and all its contents, while these friends are bound to us in turn by the same inviolable law of loyalty and trustworthiness.

Aelred explored and defended the possibility of uniquely intimate relationships that one monk might share with another, in which secrets were exchanged and depths of mutual trust were attained—the sort of relationships that didn't exist with every other monk in the monastery. True, Aelred did envision the gradual expansion of spiritual friendship, so that one's circle of trusted brothers might grow to encompass a wide community, all united by the same love that prompted the early Christians, for instance, to yield their property to one another (see Acts 2:42–47). But he maintained that that vision can only come to fruition if it begins small, with pairs or trios of committed brothers. The widening ripples of affection begin with the one pebble dropped in the pool.

It's a risky venture, in many ways—encouraging celibate monks to seek out intimacy with one another—and for that reason, Aelred has often been considered a subversive figure. In the 1950s it was forbidden at Trappist monasteries for novices to read his work on friendship. His earliest readers, not to mention his contemporary ones, recognized that he was advocating something with the potential to stoke the fires of desire. And once those flames are ablaze, there's no predicting what might happen.

The late historian John Boswell, in his *Christianity, Social Tolerance, and Homosexuality*, was in no doubt about Aelred's significance for our current dilemmas surrounding friendship: "There can be little question that Aelred was gay and that his erotic attraction to men was a dominant force in his life," Boswell writes. Accordingly, he sees in Aelred and his treatises the possibility of a Christian affirmation of gay partnerships. Aelred's writings on friendship, in Boswell's view, may be read as commendations not just of chaste, intimate same-sex relationships but also of specifically romantic partnerships between men (and, by extension, between women). Aelred becomes the patron saint of gay and lesbian love, the historical forerunner of advocates for same-sex marriage in the church today.

Whatever one makes of this line of thought—and we'll return to it in a subsequent chapter—it's significant that most who agree with Boswell admit that, although the eleventh-century abbot likely experienced what we now call a "homosexual orientation," Aelred himself was celibate. Aelred speaks in some of his writings about the dalliances in his youth and losing his virginity, the context of these remarks suggesting that he had been with a man. But by the time he wrote *On Spiritual Friendship*, he had bound himself to the teachings of the church and foresworn sexual liaisons. The man who could describe a friend as one "to whom you so join and unite yourself that you mix soul with soul" and one whom you could embrace "in the kiss of unity, with the sweetness of the Holy Spirit flowing over you" had apparently given up gay sex. What Aelred called "spiritual friendship" was a form of same-sex intimacy that sublimated or transmuted erotic passion rather than sanctioning its genital expression. In light of this, I wonder what it might look like to part ways with Aelred's largest circle of admirers today and attempt to recover the abbot's original vision. Aelred promoted an intimacy between friends that wasn't simply reducible to romantic love. But neither did he envision anything less than *brotherhood*. What might it look like to give up a suspicious reading of Aelred's agenda, at least as a thought experiment, and take him on his own terms?

஠

After his death, Aelred's model of devoted friendship did not lack for exemplars in his homeland of England. For roughly the next seven hundred years, from the medieval world on through to the early modern, certain pairs of friends would consider themselves not merely chums or pals, and also not homosexual lovers, but spiritual kin, "brothers" and (to mix metaphors) "wedded" friends. "This is an era," writes the historian Alan Bray, "where different kinds of kinship overlap, shade into one other and are not clearly distinguished from friendship." This is not the same as saying that friendship became a cover for sexual activity; rather the reverse—that much of what we today would locate primarily or solely in marriage and sexual partnerships, premodern people would have been able to find in friendships.

Bray's survey of roughly a thousand years of English history, from the time of feudal lords until the Victorians, published posthumously in 2003 as *The Friend*, began with a puzzle. He had been asked by an acquaintance to visit the chapel at Christ's College, Cambridge, and offer his professional opinion about a monument there—right beside the Communion table—that commemorated two men who were buried together in a nearby vault. The monument dated from 1684 and bore the names Sir John Finch and Sir Thomas Baines. Bas-relief sculptures of their respective heads stand above the twin stones bearing their in-scriptions, and in between the inscriptions is a cloth carved in stone, tied in a floral knot at the top. This final touch, Bray knew, was modeled on the so-called marriage knot—a similar cloth that symbolized the joining of husband and wife. Here, however, it joined two *men*, and in subsequent research Bray discovered that Finch had described his union with Baines as a *connubium*, a marriage. And their shared tomb, Bray adds with a poetic, poignant flourish, ensured for each of these Christian believers that, at the great future day of the resurrection of the body, each one's friend would be "the first figure his awakened eyes will see."

At first Bray wondered if he was seeing, as if for the first time, a long-forgotten historical precedent for modern same-sex marriage. If so, his find would no doubt land him on the cover of *Time* magazine, not to mention gay periodicals like *The Advocate*. But his next twenty years of study convinced Bray that the kind of union Finch and Baines memorialized with their tombstones was not a sexual one. It was, if anything, more historically mystifying than that: there existed still in the seventeenth century a vowed relationship of two male friends, who thereafter considered themselves spiritual kin, all the while remaining married to women.

In his book Bray draws attention to several notable features of these "wedded" friendships. The first is their religious character. For instance, at Merton College, Oxford, John Bloxham and John Whytton, who had been buried together three hundred years before Finch and Baines in Cambridge, were depicted in their monument as linked via their shared name "John" (or, in the inscription's Latin, "Johannes") to a third "Johannes," St. John the Baptist. Typically in their era, children would take their first name from their godparents. If the pattern holds in this case, then St. John is depicted as John Bloxham and John Whytton's "spiritual godfather . . . thus [rendering] each [of them] as spiritual brothers, in not a marital but a fraternal analogy." The two Johns were brothers, not by dint of their own will but in the sight of God and the communion of saints.

The way in which these spiritual unions had often been sealed in the medieval era was with a liturgy, performed in view of but also outside the doors of the church, signifying that these pacts were sanctioned by divine authority but were also folkloric in origin rather than strictly sacramental. In the Christian East, such rites, as Pavel Florensky notes, already bore a more overtly spiritual character. With *adelphōpoiēsis*, the rite of brother-making, the two friends who were making promises to each other shared Holy Communion, partaking of the presanctified elements from a common cup, and exchanged crosses with each other. After they traded kisses, the Scripture was read: "Behold,

how good and how pleasant it is for brethren to dwell together
in unity!" (Ps. 133:1 KJV). Discussing the medieval European
viewpoint that one's best friends were one's family members,
the historian Marc Bloch writes: "The general assumption was
that there was no real friendship save between persons united in
blood." But Christians stood that assumption on its head. Where
people may have been skeptical of "spiritual" ties, Christians
came to believe that the truest and most durable relationships
were friendships that were sealed with the common participation
in the Eucharistic body and blood of Christ. If blood is thicker
than water, then Eucharistic blood is thickest of all.

Later on in the Latin West, including England, such rites
sometimes (though perhaps not as often as we might wish)[2]
included a prayer like the following:

> O Lord our God Almighty, who was and is and is to come,
> who did not disdain to be born of humankind in the womb of
> the Virgin Mary Mother of God, send your holy angel upon
> these your servants [name] and [name] that they may love each
> other, as your holy apostles Peter and Paul loved each other, and
> Andrew and James, and John and Thomas, James, Philip, Mat-
> thew, Simon, Thaddeus, Matthias and your holy martyrs Sergius
> and Bacchus, Cosmas and Damian, not through the bonds of
> birth, but through faith and by the love of the Holy Spirit, and
> that they may abide in the same love all the days of their life.

The voluntary love of the two friends, birthed in them by the
Spirit rather than through biological kinship, is here recognized,
blessed, and given concrete shape. Hereafter the sworn brothers
will be known not simply by their own names but in relation to

2. Keith Thomas writes: "It is true that friendship was often described as
'holy' or 'sacred,' and that the Communion service was an acknowledged rite
of reconciliation, but it is very doubtful whether more than a tiny minority of
these close friendships had any such sacramental overtones. There is, however,
no doubting their public character or their social and emotional importance.
John Donne said that friendship was his 'second religion.'"

each other: "I am John, the friend of Thomas"; "I am Thomas, the friend of John."

And that brings us to a second notable feature of these friendship bonds that Bray discusses, which is their public, communal significance. In both medieval and early modern Europe, such ties of brotherhood served a social function. Although in the West the friendship bond mostly didn't guarantee inheritance rights, it did serve to forge an alliance between two men, as well as their families. When wars crippled, in multiple senses, those who fought in them, a sworn bond of friendship between warriors provided assurance of mutual ransom in the event of capture and guaranteed assistance and shared profits after the fact. Even in later times, during the waning of the medieval age and the so-called passage to modernity, friendship continued to play this public role, though changes began to be visible, too, as we'll see.

Friendship, in other words, belonged in the realm of law and policy, of public interest and observed give-and-take. Today we still consider private weddings—elopements and courthouse appointments and unannounced ceremonies—to be the exception rather than the norm, and many in the medieval-to-early-modern era would have said something similar about friendship. Just as we consider marriages today to be in need of a bridal party to witness and reinforce the vows the couple are taking, and also hold them to those vows when the honeymoon glow begins to dim, so pairs of friends were thought to need—and were guaranteed, whether they wanted it or not—a web of patrons, kin, and fellow church members who made sure they didn't mistake their union for a mere passing fascination.

The third notable feature of these friendships, according to Bray, is that they weren't limited to the brawny world of warriors. Women, too, took vows of friendship, albeit much less frequently and visibly. As late as the mid-nineteenth century, Anne Lister sat in her aunt's parlor in Yorkshire and confided that she would be taking Ann Walker as her lifelong companion. Walker had already told Lister that she would consider their union "as good as a marriage," to which Lister had replied, "quite as good or better."

On Easter Day, 1834, Lister and Walker knelt at the communion rail beneath the east window at Holy Trinity Church, Goodramgate, and took vows of friendship. Had they let their gaze drift upward to the window, they would have seen its fifteenth-century donor named in its panels: "Walcar . . . ioh(annis)," or "John Walker," who used to be the rector of the parish. Flanking the tiny figure of John in the stained glass were portraits of St. John the Baptist and St. John the Evangelist, two saints who shared the donor's name, as was usual for a man's godparents and spiritual family. "They are here," suggests Bray, "because they are his kindred and his friends."

Would Lister and Walker have taken all this in as they solemnized their own spiritual kinship by receiving the Eucharist together that Easter Day and exchanging promises of mutual love and devotion? Perhaps so. Then again, what they were doing—ritualizing and "fixing" (as Lister writes in her diary) their union, making their friendship "marriage-like"—was not the antique curiosity it has now become. Kneeling beneath that sunlit glass, they knew they were taking their place in a long history of vowed friendships. Presumably, they had no reason to think it abnormal.

Lister and Walker lived, however, on the cusp of great social change. In retrospect, already in the century before these two women took their vows, friendship had begun to shift from a public, tangibly beneficial relationship to a private one that had no agreed-upon aims or ends other than the continuance of the mutual attraction itself. Within a generation, relationships like the one they fortified on that nineteenth-century Easter morning would be largely a relic of the past. Henceforth, in a changed England, friendship came to be thought of, in Keith Thomas's words, as "based wholly on mutual sympathy, and cherished for its own sake rather than for its practical advantages."

This relational transformation—the gradual evolution of the friendship bond—was part and parcel of wider shifts in English life, discernible even in things like architecture. Great halls, which in former times had been the places for gentlemen to display their friendships through public gestures of affection, were gradually replaced with smaller dining rooms. The servants who waited on the diners, likewise, had begun to live in their own quarters, newly removed from the daily life of those who employed them. "A whole range of bodily activities," writes the philosopher Mark Vernon, "including eating, drinking, toilet and sleeping stopped taking place inside what might broadly be called the space of the extended household and started taking place within the much narrower confines of what might be called the 'marital space.'" The upshot of this was that the bodily intimacy—the kiss of peace between male warriors, for instance—which had formerly marked the spiritual intimacy of *friendship* now became more narrowly associated with the realm of husband and wife. Friendship was being pushed out to the margins of public life, and *marriage* was taking its place as one of the only forms of vowed kinship that society would recognize.

These shifts go a long way, I think, toward explaining the sort of reaction Eberhard Bethge received when he spoke about his intimate friendship with Dietrich Bonhoeffer. If he and Dietrich weren't married, if they weren't lovers, well then, what *were* they? The cultural category of sworn brothers, of vowed friends, had, by the time Eberhard spoke, more or less receded from view. And, as Michel Foucault shrewdly observes, that's the main reason homosexuality looms like a specter over otherwise unremarkable relationships like Dietrich and Eberhard's. "Friendship had disappeared," Foucault writes, "as a culturally accepted relation." And once that disappearance was nearly complete, only then would the issue arise as a cultural anxiety: "What is going on between men?"

Previously, in the days of people as different from one another as the eleventh-century abbot Aelred and the nineteenth-century villager Anne Lister, permanent, honored, church-sanctioned, same-sex friendships were a recognized thread of the fabric of society. But those days have passed.

ॐ

Some might say, at this point, that it's just as well we've consigned these intimate, vowed forms of friendship to the dustbin of history. When I shared some of this history with a group of Christian college students recently, one of the young women responded that she worried about the potential dangers of such relationships. She mentioned an example of an especially close friendship between two women that she'd witnessed and how it seemed ingrown, obsessive, and unhealthy. Perhaps, she concluded, Dietrich Bonhoeffer was right. Friendship, in contrast to marriage or family ties, has no publicly recognized rights (or has them *no longer*), and that's a *good* thing, after all. Do we really want to return to a time when, to borrow Alan Bray's words, different forms of kinship *overlap* and *shade* into one another? Surely there's merit in making distinctions between the love of marriage, and allowing it to have its own set of expectations, and the love of friendship, with its separable set of expectations.

Pondering all the potential dangers of the forms of friendship Bray studied, though, I find myself thinking of another danger emerging from the opposite direction. I think of the Christians I know—single and married, gay and straight, young and elderly—who are desperate for deeper friendships, and I remember the stories of their loneliness. I think of their disappointment in not being able to find as much intimate human communion in their churches as they'd hoped, and I wonder what can be done about it. From the vantage point afforded by their suffering, I find myself wondering which is the greater danger—the ever-present possibility of codependency, sexual transgression, emotional smothering (and other temptations that come with close friendship) or else the burden, not to mention the attendant temptations, of isolation and solitude created by the absence of human closeness? A great company of saints witnesses to the fact that we can indeed flourish without romance, marriage, or children; I don't know of one who witnesses to the possibility of our flourishing without love altogether.

And that's why I'm inclined to say that, for all its potential problems, what we really need today is a return to Florensky's— and Aelred's, and Alan Bray's—hope in the possibility of vowed spiritual siblinghood. What we need now isn't disinterested, disembodied companionship. We need stronger bonds between brothers and sisters in Christ. We need ways to voluntarily surrender our freedom and independence and link ourselves, spiritually and tangibly, to those we've come to love.

The Catholic writer and activist Maggie Gallagher describes two kinds of relationships. To the first she gives the tagline, "You're mine because I love you." In this kind of relationship, you and I may belong to a special friendship and share many of the joys that that kind of friendship makes possible. But such joys will last only as long as my love lasts. If I tire of you or am hurt by you, I'm free to walk away—no obligations, no hoops to jump through, no strings attached. You only belong to me if I can keep up my love for you, and you can keep up yours for me. We thus dance on the precipice of loss.

On the other hand, Gallagher talks about a different sort of relationship. To this one she gives a tagline that's the inverse of her first: "I love you because you're mine." In this latter type of friendship, my love for you isn't the basis of our connection. It's the other way around: we are bound to each other, and therefore I love you. You may still bore me or wound me or otherwise become unattractive to me, but that doesn't mean

I'll walk away. You're not mine because I love you; I love you because you're—already, and always—mine. We've made promises to each other; we've committed to each other, in the sight of our families and our churches, and in the strength of those vows, I will, God willing, go on loving you.[3]

What would it mean to see friendship—specifically Christian friendship, the kind we want to strengthen and nurture in our churches—as more of the second kind of relationship than the first? What would it mean if we made promises to each other, precisely *as friends*?

৪১

The people I described in the opening paragraphs of this chapter—including me—are hungry for more than just the possibility of (to use an image from C. S. Lewis that we'll return to in a later chapter) standing shoulder to shoulder with others around a roaring fire, no matter how inviting its warmth. We are eager for our friends to say to us, "I love you because you're mine," without leaving themselves an escape clause. When I read about Eberhard Bethge wanting the prison guards to recognize and respect his unique relationship to Dietrich Bonhoeffer, I understand exactly what he's after. What I and others like me are yearning for isn't just a weekly night out or a circle of people with whom to go on vacation. We need something more. We need people who know what time our plane lands, who will worry about us when we don't show up at the time we said we would. We need people we can call and tell about that funny thing that happened in the hallway after class. We need the assurance that, come hell or high water, a few people will stay with us, loving us in spite of our faults and caring for us when we're down. More than that, we need people for whom *we* can

3. I think here of Dietrich Bonhoeffer's words about what marriage vows accomplish: "It is not your love that upholds marriage, but from now on it is marriage that upholds your love."

care. (As another single friend of mine put it recently, you want to be able to make soup for friends who are sick, not just have someone who will make soup for you when you're sick. In the absence of mutually recognized commitments, it's not always clear that that kind of reciprocity is welcome.)

And, again, these needs aren't limited to singles. I know two married couples in their twenties who recently decided to share a large house. One of the couples has a small child, and the wife of the other couple said to me, "Living together, I see more clearly how raising kids was never meant to be something two parents do on their own." Being a young mother or father can be among the most isolating experiences in our fragmented contemporary culture, and what young parents need—perhaps above all—is the devotion of close friends who won't bail when the dirty diapers and the spit-up and the nighttime cries become overwhelming.

In short, we need our friendship ties to shade into and perhaps even overlap with our ties of brotherhood and sisterhood, of marriage and kinship.

I believe that recovering the historic Christian practice of vowed friendships can help with all these needs. Certainly such friendships will have to look different than they did in Aelred of Rievaulx or Pavel Florensky's day. I hardly expect my Anglican church, for instance, to get excited about the Orthodox rite of *adelphōpoiēsis*, or "brother-making," anytime soon (as much as I might wish for that!). But if we translate the practice of committed, promise-bound friendships into our time, we can retrieve some of the wisdom of those relationships and apply it afresh in our own changed contexts. This will, of course, require imagination and an ability to improvise. I can't kneel at a communion rail and make vows to my friend under stained-glass-tinted Easter morning sunbeams. But I can learn from historical precedents and look for ways to reclaim their benefits in my own cultural contexts. With the help of my fellow Christians, I hope, at least, that I can.

ℬ

A few years ago, I was washing dishes at my house in England when the phone rang. I mopped the suds from my hands and answered. It was my friend Jono. Would I consider, he asked, being his daughter Callie's godfather, a witness to her baptism and a help to her parents as they sought to raise her in the Christian faith?

"Think and pray about it," Jono suggested.

I felt honored and—instantaneously—drawn deeper into the circle of his and his wife Megan's friendship.

Several weeks later, I stood near the baptismal font in a small Anglican church, warmed by the cascade of sunlight pouring through the windows behind me. The priest lifted Callie, dressed in her new white dress, above the font, dipped his hand in the water, and made the sign of the cross on her forehead. "Parents and godparents," the priest said, "the church receives Callie with joy. Today we are trusting God for her growth in faith. Will you pray for her, draw her by your example into the community of faith, and walk with her in the way of Christ?" Alongside Callie's godmothers, I answered, "With the help of God, we will."

It wasn't an exchange of vows between a friend and me—at least not directly. Nonetheless, it was close to that. Becoming a godparent meant that my relationship to two of my good friends, and their children, had been sealed through baptism and witnessed by a fellowship of believers. It was a small step toward the transformation of a "You're mine because I love you" relationship into an "I love you because you're mine" relationship. A small step, but hopefully the first of many on a long journey.

3

The Transformation
of Friendship

No longer do I call you servants, for the servant does
not know what his master is doing; but I have called you
friends, for all that I have heard from my Father I have
made known to you.

—Jesus (John 15:15)

Christians think differently about friendship because their
understanding of friendship is rooted not in rosy accounts
of human perfectibility but in a God who remains ever
faithful to us and who never, no matter how egregious our
failings, writes us out of the story of divine love.

—Paul Wadell

A few years ago I gave a talk in which I sketched some of
the cultural history I've laid out in the previous two
chapters. I discussed how, compared to what it was in
the Christian past, friendship has become a weak bond that is

often sidelined in our rush to celebrate romantic love. I went on, though, about how I feel hopeful that individual Christians and churches can recover some of friendship's previous honor and look for ways in our own time to strengthen it. Afterward, during the question-and-answer session, one of the audience members raised his hand and asked, "Where in the Bible would you direct someone who wanted to see some scriptural support for what you're saying?" It was, of course, precisely the right question to ask.

Scripture-reading Christians have a complicated relationship with the ideal of intimate friendship. In the Protestant tradition, at least, there is a long history of suspicion being directed toward the relationship. Many interpreters have pointed out how the New Testament grew out of a world in which friendship—or at least a particular understanding of friendship—was prized and esteemed. Aristotle had allotted two whole chapters of his ten-chapter *Nicomachean Ethics* to discussing friendship, and he spoke for many in his era when he maintained that the highest and noblest forms of friendship were preferential and exclusive: you were a friend because you were singled out to be one, chosen for your attainments, whether material or moral. You could not, in Aristotle's view, be friends with a slave unless you were yourself a slave. And as for friendship between the sexes, Aristotle included it in his discussion of how friendship between unequal partners may partake of virtue, albeit only partially. Likewise, many of Cicero's ideals about the necessity of friends occupying the same social status and the precise nature of the bond that knit them together had permeated the Greco-Roman culture of the first century. "In the classical understanding," Steve Summers concludes, "reciprocity was a prime feature of friendship, having within it implications of equal standing and material parity, so that it could not be limited to the conceptual level of virtue and character."

Perhaps here is the best place to sketch a brief history of friendship, from the ancient Greeks and Romans up to the time of the New Testament, in the hope that the Christian vision can be seen for the strikingly original force that it was. Prior to Jesus, the classical world celebrated friendship, adorning its literature with depictions of friends' valiant exploits. In the eighth century BCE, Homer's distinctive take on the story of the Trojan War hero Achilles and his friend Patroclus in *The Iliad* bequeathed to subsequent minstrels and artists a stockpile of images and dialogue to draw on. "Patroklos, whom I loved beyond all other companions," Achilles says at his friend's death. "There is nothing worse than this I could suffer, not even if I were to hear of the death of my father . . . or the death of my dear son." This grief gives Achilles the final push he needs to return to the battlefield, and thus the memory of this particular friendship is intimately bound up with Achilles's own stature as a triumphing champion.

Other pairs in the ancient world received virtually identical acclaim. Theseus, the mythic founder of the city of Athens, hymned by Ovid and other poets, was linked to Pirithous in devout friendship. The two had originally met on the battlefield, to settle a score, but their mutual admiration led them to make a pact instead, and their subsequent commitment to each other was held up as a model for others.

Orestes and Pylades were lauded with similar accolades. Orestes had been commissioned by the god Apollo to steal an image of Artemis. Iphigenia, Orestes's sister and a priestess of Artemis, ordered him killed when he arrived on her shores, but she was unable to discern who was Orestes and who was Pylades, since each, seeking to spare the other the death sentence, claimed to be Orestes. Commenting on a dramatization of this story, Cicero wrote, "The audience rose to its feet and applauded at this fictional scene. What do we think they would have done if it had been real?"

Damon and Pythias, to take one more example, were also prepared to follow each other to death, if need be, in the course of their
friendship. The fourth-century CE author Iamblichus portrays
Pythias, having been condemned to face execution by the emperor,
asking Damon to serve as hostage in his stead so that he can set
his affairs in order. Damon consents to do so—which would be
shocking enough—but Pythias, rather than seizing the opportunity Damon has given him to escape, honors his commitment and
returns to free his friend and accept his sentence. The emperor, in
awe of this loyalty, asks to enter the circle of their friendship too,
but the two men refuse. The pair remains unbroken.

It wasn't only stories of friendship that captured the ancient
imagination. More abstract, theoretical treatments, such as Aristotle's—to which we now return—served as patterns that could
be bandied about, followed as a rule book, or modified depending on the particular exigencies of culture and community. In the
Nicomachean Ethics, Aristotle recognized the natural affinities
that form between people born in the same locale or sharing
characteristics such as upbringing and education, and he valued
those connections. He had no vested interest in dismissing the
importance of pleasant but shallow neighborly relations—those
relations help keep the worlds of home, market, and government
tolerably humane. But, fundamentally, he thought certain forms
of friendship were more valuable than others. Friendships could
be traced to three sources—mutual benefit or advantage, pleasure, or character formation—and Aristotle left no doubt that
the latter was the most prized. In a friendship based on a shared
pursuit of virtue, friends "love each other *for themselves*"—for
who they each *are*, not for what they stand to gain. As Gilbert
Meilaender summarizes, in Aristotle's view, friendship "is a
narrowing down of the many toward whom we have good will
to a few friends whom we especially choose."

Against this backdrop, some Protestant Christians have de-
tected a thinly disguised polemic against friendship in the pages

of the New Testament. When in the ancient Greek and Roman worlds "friendships were the noblest things in the world," the Anglican divine Jeremy Taylor stated bluntly, at exactly that cultural moment "charity was little." In other words, when the world around them gave honor to pairs of noblemen and warriors, the apostles instead established the universal, indiscriminate love of *enemies* as the apex of Christian virtue. *Agape*, not *philia*, was the characteristic Christian virtue.

This line of thought is evident in Christian writers as different from one another as Samuel Johnson, the maker of the great forerunner to the *Oxford English Dictionary*; Søren Kierkegaard, the acerbic Danish Christian philosopher; and Karl Barth, the Swiss preacher, professor, and one of the twentieth century's greatest Reformed theologians (to name just a few). For his part, Kierkegaard maintained that Christian love does "not make distinctions," selecting one class of people (friends) for special affection while leaving others (enemies, acquaintances, the faceless "rest") outside the circle of preferment. "The Christian love-command requires one to love God above all and then to love one's neighbour," Kierkegaard wrote. "In love and friendship preference is the middle term; in love to one's neighbour God is the middle term." He went on: "Let the poet search the New Testament for a word about friendship which could please him, and he will search vainly unto despair." Johnson concurred: "All friendship is preferring the interest of a friend, to the neglect, or, perhaps, against the interest of others. . . . Now Christianity recommends universal benevolence, to consider all men as our brethren; which is contrary to the virtue of friendship, as described by the ancient philosophers." And Karl Barth, in his inimitably symphonic prose, softens the picture a bit but ends up with a similar conclusion:

> The Christian does not like all his fellows, not even all his fellow-Christians. But he likes some of them and he is ready

to do a good deal, perhaps the very greatest things, to please them. May he continue to do so, and may what he does on this presupposition be to the benefit of both parties! But although Christian love for the neighbour and brother does not exclude this presupposition—it may indeed be realised on this presupposition—it is not in any way tied to it.

Fortified by this line of reasoning, many Christians have not been able to find much of an endorsement for friendship in the pages of Scripture.

And yet the *vocabulary* of friendship is there, even on the lips of Jesus in the Fourth Gospel, as we saw in the last chapter: "No one has greater love than this, that someone would lay down his life for his friends" (John 15:13, my translation). Proverbs, likewise, celebrates the bond of friendship, a bond that, apparently, can be even more meaningful than that between siblings (18:24). Its simple summary statement is lapidary: "A friend loves at all times" (17:17).

Furthermore, there are exemplars of apparently exclusive pairs of friends in the Bible, especially the Old Testament. One classic instance is found in the book of Ruth, which tells the story of the widow Naomi's decision to return to Judah, her native homeland. After her husband's and then her two sons' deaths, there is little reason to remain in Moab any longer. Ruth, however, a Moabite woman whom one of Naomi's sons had married, refuses to let Naomi return by herself. She flouts the traditional expectations of kinship (normally a woman in her situation would have returned to her own family, as Naomi observes [1:8–9]) and insists that she belongs with her mother-in-law rather than with her own biological mother. In language strongly reminiscent of marriage vows, Ruth promises Naomi, "Where you go I will go, and where you lodge I will lodge. Your people shall be my people, and your God my God" (1:16). (Shades of various kinship relationships blurring together again—was this a kind of "wedded friendship"?) And then, recalling our discussion of shared tombs in the last chapter, Ruth says to Naomi, "Where you die I will die, and there will I be buried. May the LORD do so to me and more also if anything but death parts me from you" (1:17). The story concludes with Ruth unexpectedly finding a Judahite husband and bearing a son, Obed. This denouement is telling, because it is the narrator's way of giving Ruth and Naomi's friendship an elevated place in the history of salvation: Obed, Ruth's son, becomes the grandfather of David, Israel's greatest king. As Steve Summers observes, "Here, *friendship* is seen as the means by which the Davidic line is established." If you know your Old Testament history, you'll know that's an elevated status for friendship indeed.

Perhaps unsurprisingly, then, Ruth's great-grandson David himself becomes one of the Old Testament's other primary exemplars of friendship, described in a story as brief as it is moving. (The David and Jonathan story, says Pavel Florensky, "is depicted in just a few words, but for that [is] almost painfully touching: 'Written as if for me,' everyone thinks.") Meeting initially as fellow warriors on the battlefield, David and Jonathan forge a covenantal friendship, complete with an exchange of gifts and mutual promises:

> As soon as he had finished speaking to Saul, the soul of Jonathan was knit to the soul of David, and Jonathan loved him as his own soul. And Saul took him that day and would not let him return to his father's house. Then Jonathan made a covenant with David, because he loved him as his own soul. And Jonathan stripped himself of the robe that was on him and gave it to David, and his armor, and even his sword and his bow and his belt. (1 Sam. 18:1–4)

Subsequently, David marries Jonathan's sister, and the bond between them is thereby further solidified. When Saul, David's new father-in-law, grows jealous and attempts to assassinate David, Jonathan intervenes to rescue him. Knowing that his friend must flee, Jonathan arranges one last meeting with David, at which "they kissed one another and wept with one another, David weeping the most" (1 Sam. 20:41). Years later, upon learning of Jonathan's death, David laments: "I am distressed for you, my brother Jonathan; very pleasant have you been to me; your love to me was extraordinary, surpassing the love of women" (2 Sam. 1:26).

Various biblical scholars have, on the one hand, downplayed the emotional intensity of David's words. After all, it is sometimes said, Jonathan's "love" for David was only a generic accolade that echoed the people of Israel's acclaim for their new king; it was more a political phenomenon than anything else—not really "friendship" at all in our modern sense of the word. On the other hand, more progressive readers of Scripture have sometimes taken the opposite strategy and argued that David and Jonathan were lovers, investing David's lament over his friend's dead body with a backstory of sexual liaisons and erotic passion. Neither of these pathways has proved persuasive to most biblical scholars, who point out that often in Scripture—as is the case in the history we surveyed in the previous chapter—the language of nonsexual friendship and romantic love are vocabularies that can overlap and intermingle. Probably David borrowed the language and imagery of spousal love, just as Ruth did before him, to describe a relationship that wasn't sexually active but was, nonetheless, more intense, more committed and irrevocable, than most moderns consider friendship to be.

The same pattern arguably holds in the New Testament, not least in the case of Jesus himself. Again, in the Gospel of John, Jesus is portrayed as the friend of Lazarus. Lazarus is "he whom you love," his sister Mary says to Jesus (11:3). A little later, turning to his disciples (among whom, apparently, Lazarus isn't numbered), Jesus calls Lazarus simply "our friend"

(11:11). When Lazarus dies, Jesus visits his grave and, upon seeing the grief of his relatives and community, becomes "deeply moved in his spirit and greatly troubled" (11:33). And then the text says with devastating, tantalizing understatement, "Jesus wept." It is telling that when we catch a glimpse of the depth of Jesus's emotions—which we rarely do in the Gospels—we see a portrayal of his sadness at the death of a *friend*, one who is bound to him not in a relationship of traveling companion, student, patron, or lover but only by ties of affection. The only tears of Jesus that are reported in the Gospels are prompted by the loss of one of his same-sex friends. As someone I know has put it, "Love wept at the grave of his friend."

Armed with this kind of evidence, certain Christians have tried to make the case that a theology of friendship is, in fact, to be found in the Bible—and not just found but honored, promoted, and sanctified. The great nineteenth-century English convert to Roman Catholicism, John Henry Newman, for instance, took pen in hand to oppose the views of Kierkegaard, Samuel Johnson, and others who believed that friendship was out of step with Christian ethics. Focusing again on the Fourth Gospel and highlighting its portrayal of one disciple whom Jesus evidently loved with a particularly noteworthy devotion (John 13:23; 19:26; 20:2; 21:7, 20), Newman wrote in a sermon:

> Much might be said on this remarkable circumstance. I say *remarkable*, because it might be supposed that the Son of God Most High could not have loved one man more than another; or again, if so, that He would not have had only one friend, but, as being All-holy, He would have loved all men more or less, in proportion to their holiness. Yet we find our Saviour had a private friend; and this shows us, first, how entirely He was a man, as much as any of us, in His wants and feelings; and next, that there is nothing contrary to the spirit of the Gospel, nothing inconsistent with the fulness of Christian love, in having our affections directed in an especial way towards certain objects,

towards those whom the circumstances of our past life, or some peculiarities of character, have endeared to us.

Newman went further, however. Not only was it permissible to have such a friend; it was something that should be positively encouraged and commended, since particular friendships have the potential to induct us into patterns of self-giving and hospitality that we might otherwise fail to learn if we hold ourselves to abstractions like "loving humanity" or even "loving our enemies."

> There have been men before now, who have supposed Christian love was so diffusive as not to admit of concentration upon individuals; so that we ought to love all men equally. And many there are, who, without bringing forward any theory, yet consider practically that the love of many is something superior to the love of one or two; and neglect the charities of private life, while busy in the schemes of an expansive benevolence, or of effecting a general union and conciliation among Christians. Now I shall here maintain, in opposition to such notions of Christian love, and with our Saviour's pattern [of loving Lazarus and the so-called "Beloved Disciple"] before me, that the best preparation for loving the world at large, and loving it duly and wisely, is to cultivate an intimate friendship and affection towards those who are immediately about us.

If you're committed to letting the Bible, and above all the life of Jesus, shape your ethics, it's hard to argue with Newman's reasoning. The testimony of the Fourth Gospel seems indisputable: Jesus had a sort of "best," or closest, friend. When an acquaintance of Samuel Johnson, a Quaker woman named Mrs. Knowles, confronted Johnson with reasoning that was very similar to Newman's—"But, Doctor, our Saviour had twelve Apostles, yet there was *one* whom he *loved*"—the great writer was forced to concede: "Very well, indeed, Madam. You have said very well." Johnson's companion James Boswell, stunned by Johnson's concession, asked him, "Pray, Sir, had you ever thought of it?" "I had not," Johnson admits. (Newly converted to Mrs. Knowles's perspective, Johnson didn't, however, want to take it too far: "I am willing to love all mankind, *except an American.*")

&

The New Testament—or more precisely, the good news of Jesus Christ proclaimed in its pages—does make possible the kind of vowed, committed, sibling-like friendships I've been suggesting we can recover. But it doesn't just do this by laying out examples, such as Jesus and Lazarus, and then turning us loose to follow or else discard those examples depending on our whim or ability. Rather, I want to suggest, the New Testament portrays a movement or dynamic, initiated in the ministry of Jesus himself and propelled forward in the life and witness of the apostles Paul and John and others, that catches us up in its wake, empowering us to have friendships we wouldn't otherwise be able to seek or find. There is something happening, the Gospels suggest, that compels us to pursue friendships, rather than just leaving them available, as something we can take or leave. "The kingdom of God is at hand," Jesus announces, and nothing—including our human relationships—can ever be the same (Mark 1:14–15).

When Jesus is asked about his understanding of kinship and familial ties, he doesn't reject them as so much detritus from the old regime that his kingdom is displacing. Instead, he takes the basic notion of "family" and cracks it open, stretches its contents beyond their agreed-upon limits, and wraps the result around a much wider range of people than was socially acceptable. Once, when he was teaching, his mother and brothers arrived, expecting him to part the crowds and seat them within earshot. His disciples even told him as much: "Your mother and your brothers are outside, seeking you" (Mark 3:32). To which he retorted, "Who are my mother and my brothers?" (v. 33). This rhetorical question amounts, within the frame of first-century Jewish culture, to what Julie Hanlon Rubio has called a "radical rejection of the traditional family." In its place Jesus substitutes a "restructured family and community life in which disciple-ship had priority for all": "And looking about at those who sat around him, he said, 'Here are my mother and my brothers! Whoever does the will of God, he is my brother and sister and mother'" (vv. 34–35). You *will* have close relationships if you follow me, Jesus seems to say. They will just look different from what you originally envisioned.

This widening of family ties required Jesus's earliest follow-ers to redescribe what it was they were doing in their traipsing around Judea with him. Perhaps at one time, or even on an ongoing basis, they were tempted to view their discipleship in purely negative terms. They had left their fishing nets behind; they had forsaken their biological kin; they had abandoned their former markers of social identity. But in light of Jesus's teaching, they learned to renarrate those choices in positive terms, so that whatever potential losses they incurred in heeding Jesus's call were, from their new perspective, gains. The disciples weren't orphans or pariahs as they hiked along with Jesus in Galilee and, ultimately, joined him on his final journey to Jerusalem. They were adoptees—given, by Jesus, an entirely new set of parents, siblings, and cousins, brought into a new circle of kin and spiritual relations. In a sense, they were made friends of one another. When Peter, at one point, lapsed back into a trumpet-ing of his own great sacrifices for the cause ("See, we have left everything and followed you" [Mark 10:28]), Jesus quickly cut him off: "Truly, I say to you, there is no one who has left house or brothers or sisters or mother or father or children or lands, for my sake and for the gospel, who will not receive a hundredfold now in this time, houses and brothers and sisters and mothers and children and lands, with persecutions, and in the age to come eternal life" (Mark 10:29–30). Peter had to be taught that discipleship isn't a life of focusing on what's lost; the friends, siblings, and spiritual parents Peter was surrounded by were the *rewards* of discipleship that he couldn't afford to ignore.

Following along in Jesus's wake, Paul too relativized biological ties in order to elevate the new spiritual siblinghood that he understood the death and resurrection of Jesus to have created. "For as many of you as were baptized into Christ have put on Christ," Paul writes, picturing baptism as something that clothes believers with identical Christ-shaped garments and constitutes them henceforth as one another's kin (Gal. 3:27). Because of their submersion in the same baptismal waters, they were "all one in Christ Jesus" (Gal. 3:28). "For in one Spirit we were all baptized into one body—Jews or Greeks, slaves or free—and all were made to drink of one Spirit" (1 Cor. 12:13). For that reason, Paul used the language of "brothers and sisters" to characterize the relationships that all the baptized enjoyed with one another. "These bonds go deeper and demand more of us by way of solidarity than any others, even than those of family," writes Paul Griffiths. "The bonds of citizenship [and biological kinship] are to them as cotton thread is to a steel hawser." And in this conviction, Jesus and Paul are one.

Gradually, then, the ancient ideal of friendship, as it was articulated by Aristotle, Cicero, and others, wasn't so much abandoned in the early church (as Kierkegaard thought) as it was transformed. Bent into a peculiar new configuration by the advent of Jesus and the descent of God's Spirit, friendship was now shaped by the cross and the empty tomb. No longer would believers gravitate only toward their social equals; now they would form committed, permanent relationships of affection that cut across lines of enslaved versus free, wealthy versus poor, highborn versus peasant. And what they found when they traversed these boundaries was a social cohesion built not so much around the pursuit of "virtues," in the classical sense, but rather around the aim of conformity to the humiliated and exalted Christ. "Christian friendship," according to Stephen Fowl, "[was] founded on a common baptism, on common membership in Christ's body." It was centered on the quest, as Paul put it, "to know him and the power of his resurrection and the fellowship of his sufferings, becoming conformed to his death" (Phil. 3:10, my translation).

Friendship among believers, from the time of Paul onward, would therefore be understood as fundamentally a relationship between spiritual kin, with a cruciform telos. As one late fourth-century Christian writer said in a letter to a friend,

> For [our friendship] is not as a secular friendship, which is often begotten more in hope than in faith, but rather that spiritual kind, which is produced by God as its source and is joined in a brotherhood of souls. Consequently, it does not develop toward love by daily familiarity nor does it depend on anticipation of proof but, as is worthy of a daughter of truth, it is born at once stable and great, because it arises out of fullness through Christ.

Friendship, then, is not simply endorsed by the good news of God in Christ but is also *redefined* by it and redirected toward wider, deeper ends. I think, for instance, of the way the peace activist and theologian William Stringfellow described his relationship with Anthony Towne: "Our acquaintance became friendship, then, eventually, community." In other words, the two couldn't stay cocooned and turned in on themselves; in their commitment to trumpeting the nonviolent way of Christ, the two became three, and then four and five. . . .

The story of Jesus's self-giving for the sake of sinners inevitably exerts pressure on our understanding of friendship, pushing us out beyond comfortably narrow boundaries of affection and expanding our love to include others whom, previously, we would have left outside our charmed circle. This, surely, explains why Jesus says the love of friendship is the greatest of all loves— not because he is setting it over *against* the love of enemies or love of the world at large but rather because he is imagining a self-giving kind of friendship that considers even enemies to be one's potential brothers and sisters.[1] And having widened our scope, Jesus's life, death, and resurrection drive us deeper, urge us to cultivate a more profound sort of intimacy with our new friends than we would have, left to our own devices.

ॐ

Recently I was video chatting with some old friends in England. They had just had their second child and were remarking on how their fellow church members were bringing meals and helping with household chores and offering general support. "We couldn't have survived these last few weeks without that," they told me.

None of this struck me as surprising or remarkable—after all, I'd been a part of their church, and I knew people there were committed to caring for one another—until my friends recounted a conversation they'd had with another couple they knew from outside the church. Also new parents themselves, that couple expressed their astonishment at the network of support my friends enjoyed. "How do you know so many people?" they asked, incredulous. "How do you have so many friends? I wish we had half as much help as you're receiving. We have

---

1. Here is Paul D. O'Callaghan's explanation: "Jesus [in John 15:13] clearly identifies giving one's life for one's friends as the highest possible form of love. Why? Perhaps it is because giving one's life for a friend is an act of love that is formed and carried out within the communion of love. Giving one's life for a stranger might be heroic and valiant, but it does not arise from the bosom of love as such would for a friend. There is no 'greater love' because no other act of self-giving would carry the same abundance of love. Giving one's life for a friend embodies the force and dynamism of love in a way that could not be for a stranger or enemy."

friends we go to the pub with, but we don't have *any* friends who brought us meals after our baby was born."

An exchange like this gives me pause. It confronts me with the question of whether the relationships my friends enjoy—in which meals are prepared, help is given and received—are best described as "friendships" at all. From the other couple's perspective, Chris and Hannah's church network seems more *familial* than *friendly*. It seems more like a circle of siblings than a network of acquaintances.

In the New Testament, as we've seen, familial language far outweighs the language of friendship when it comes to describing Christian community. Believers are one another's "brothers and sisters in Christ," not (primarily) one another's "friends." It's true, as Stephen Fowl and others have shown, that some of the classical Greco-Roman language of friendship is reappropriated in the New Testament as descriptive for the church. But by relocating that language into a context of spiritual kinship, the New Testament reconfigures it. "Friendship" is elevated to something more than simply the sort of relationship that leads to a night at the pub; it becomes, instead, a way of speaking about the bonds between Christian siblings.

It may be, then, that part of our task in rediscovering and reinvigorating Christian friendship in our various contemporary contexts now is learning to reject certain forms of anemic "friendship" altogether. We Christians don't care too much about "friendship" if it only means having acquaintances with whom to have drinks. (Friendships based on pleasure are nice enough, of course, if you can find them, but even Aristotle recognized their dimness compared to the beauty of deeper relationships.) We do, however, care enormously about cultivating the sorts of relational ties that my friends in England enjoy—and we care about making sure their neighbors know they're welcome to come enjoy those same bonds of connections for themselves.

In short, we believe in friendship's transformation by the good news of God in Christ. We believe the gospel propels and gives a new shape to friendship, disrupting its normal modus operandi and replacing it with a new Christ-shaped agenda. We believe that our two become three, and then four and five, as we learn to recognize our kin—our brothers and sisters and mothers and fathers, as Jesus said to Peter—in the faces of our fellow believers.

In her memoir *Girl Meets God*, Lauren Winner writes about her move back to the United States to start graduate school:

> The day before I left Cambridge for good, I saw Paul and Gillian, two of the most annoying of the annoying Christians, on Clare bridge, and I hugged them. I said I would miss them. I thought I was lying, to be polite. But I wasn't. I have missed them. I do. No one else I ever meet will have pledged to support me in my life of Christ, which is exactly what Paul and Gillian pledged at my baptism. My friends at Columbia, the friends I meet for drinks at trendy bars in the Village, the friends with whom I chat about post-structuralism and Derrida—those people didn't witness my baptism. They didn't cheer at my confirmation, they didn't pray with me every Sunday for two years, they didn't hand me Kleenex when I burst into inexplicable tears in the middle of the Lord's Prayer. They aren't my brothers and sisters in Christ. They are merely my friends.

That is the transformation Christianity brought—not so much the abandonment of friendship as its revolution and redemption. The good news of God in Christ took friendships based on preference and a pursuit of social status and made them about self-giving love. It took fellow citizens, acquaintances in the great societal circle, and made them brothers and sisters. After Christ, friendship would never be the same.

PART 2

LIVING FRIENDSHIP

4

"A Piece of Ice Held Fast in the Fist"

We cannot imagine existing in our culture without the haven of an erotic partnership, because our capacity to belong together in more chaste ways is so limited.

—Christopher C. Roberts

Chastity does not mean abstention from sexual wrong; it means something flaming, like Joan of Arc.

—G. K. Chesterton

Several years ago, shortly after my book about being gay and Christian was published, I had my first meeting with one of my readers (a rite of passage for authors, I suppose). This reader—I'll call him Conor—contacted me on Facebook, through some mutual friends, and we struck up a correspondence, tentative at first but gradually more honest and self-disclosing. An undergraduate at the time, Conor reminded me of myself when I was his age: devoutly Christian, fluent in the languages of Scripture and prayer, and also clearly convinced his same-sex attraction wasn't an oscillating, ephemeral thing that would change with enough fasting and intercession. And this mix of circumstances left him anxious. He knew, or thought he knew, what he believed, which was the same set of convictions I'd advocated in my book: that marriage is intended for one man and one woman and that he, therefore, ought to be celibate, barring some unforeseen seismic shift.

When we met in person, talking on the short hike to Minnehaha Falls in Minneapolis, Conor had come to realize that he'd fallen in love with his best friend, a guy. And he told me that as he pictured the future—a stretch of years, gradually unfolding like the pleats of an expanding accordion—he visualized the same scenario playing itself out again and again. Just at the moment when his male friendships became cherished and irreplaceable, he would find himself romantically attached to those same friends, helpless to chart a way back to being just good brotherly comrades, with cooler passions. Regardless of whether his friends were gay or straight, Conor imagined himself, over and over, landing in the same place: wanting more intimacy than his friends could give and, as a result, being filled with unrequited longing and loneliness, and—probably ultimately—back to where he started at the beginning, which is to say, without anyone at all whom he could dearly cherish and be cherished by in return. "Falling in love is one of the worst things that could happen to a gay [Christian] person [who's trying to be celibate]," says the gay Christian writer Matthew Vines, "because you will necessarily be heartbroken, you will have to run away, and that will happen every single time that you come to care about someone else too much."

As Conor and I sat down on a rock near the base of the falls, we stopped talking and just listened to the slippery, cracking roar of the water. By that point, I had already suggested some possible theological perspectives on his questions. I'd told him more about my own singleness and loneliness, and we'd talked about Aelred of Rievaulx and Alan Bray and the possibility of somehow renewing vowed siblinghood in contemporary culture. But there didn't seem to be much more to say, especially when I could tell from his eyes that theology wasn't helping in that moment. I knew Conor was thinking of his friend and doubting whether what we'd said on the hike down to the falls about spiritual friendship and celibacy was really practicable at all.

℘

Probably the most commonly repeated conclusion (or assumption) in most of the reading I've done on friendship is that friendship is something completely separable from romantic or erotic love. Where romantic love is dizzyingly, deliriously all-absorbing, in friendship cooler heads prevail. Where romantic lovers tumble into a pleasure that eclipses everything and everyone else, friends select one another for their admirable qualities and virtues and take time to get to know, and to strengthen, one another's character. Romantic love, as Allan Bloom notes, describing the tumultuous relationship of Romeo and Juliet—a relationship that began as quickly and unpredictably as Romeo fell out of love with Rosaline, just a scene or two before—is "a kind of possession," whereas friendship "is a consequence of deliberate choice," unencumbered by the blind tumble of passion and appetite. "Friendship," Bloom concludes, "is human, while love is divine."

In evangelical Christian circles, the treatment of friendship that has probably been most acclaimed for making a similar case is C. S. Lewis's classic essay on friendship in his book *The Four Loves*, originally published in 1960. In that book, Lewis takes pains to distinguish friendship sharply from erotic attachment.

In contrast to lovers, whom we picture face-to-face, exchanging vows, friends are side-by-side, engaged in some common task and needing to know very little of each other's life outside the friendship. This, in Lewis's view, is friendship's true glory: "the exquisite arbitrariness and irresponsibility of this love." Lewis notes that, unlike erotic partners who are absorbed in each other's faces, each friend can say to the other, "I have no duty to be anyone's Friend and no man in the world has a duty to be mine." That shocking lack of utility—friendship isn't *for* anything in particular, such as procreation or productivity—is precisely what makes friendship itself.[1]

For Lewis, the love between friends "ignores not only our physical bodies but that whole embodiment which consists of our family, job, past and connections." Friendship, in this perspective, is "an affair of disentangled, or stripped, minds." You picture him with, say, his friend J. R. R. Tolkien or his fellow author Owen Barfield, sharing a pint at the pub and discussing some scrap of Old English literature. Beyond the jocularity and camaraderie of that moment, there need be no "relationship": the conversation itself *just is* the friendship.

It's a vision of friendship that perhaps makes most sense to someone in Lewis's shoes. For a highly educated male in mid-twentieth-century England, who couldn't rely on women for the same level of education, and for whom any awareness of homoerotic yearnings would have had to remain publicly unspoken and hidden for professional and societal reasons, it makes sense to define friendship as cleanly separable from romantic love. That was Lewis's own experience, and the friendships he managed to cultivate reinforced his belief in the pleasures such experience had to offer.

1. Lewis, who so often sounds like an emissary from the medieval world to the modern, is here a child of the seventeenth century. It was Francis Bacon, not Aelred or Cicero, who said, "It is friendship, when a man can say to himself, I love this man without respect of utility."

Lewis's reasons for sealing off friendship and romance aren't, however, the only reasons to uphold such a separation. Other Christians have followed the same path but have done so mainly in response to the growing acceptance—and celebration—of homosexuality in the modern West. When some evangelical Anglicans crafted a pastoral paper regarding gay partnerships in the church and included a commendation of chaste friendship for gay people, the theologian Gerald Bray reacted with extreme caution. "To suggest, however obliquely, that friendship can be a homosexual substitute for marriage," Bray maintained, "is dangerous and potentially destructive of the whole concept." Bray was responding to what he feared to be a dangerous implication of certain Christian discussions of celibacy and friendship among gay people: if friendship is the place where some celibate gay Christians will try to invest their love, won't that somehow taint or transform friendship into a form of erotic love—the very thing friendship ought not to be confused with, if it is to remain *friendship*? If friendship becomes a solution to loneliness, won't that make it edge ever closer toward becoming just another form of romance, all the more complicated because it's calling itself "friendship"?

Another conservative writer, Anthony Esolen, voiced similar worries in an essay he titled, plaintively, "A Requiem for Friendship." There he argued, among other things, that the only way for actions such as Abraham Lincoln's practice as a young man of sharing a bed with another male friend to remain and be considered chaste is if any hint of homosexuality is anathema from the outset. "The stigma against sodomy," Esolen writes, "cleared away ample space for an emotionally powerful friendship that did not involve sexual intercourse, exactly as the stigma against incest allows for the physical and emotional freedom of a family." Esolen's essay is a lament for a changed culture, one in which every intimate friendship is now under suspicion for being "really" romantic.

These kinds of objections gain credibility, or at least become more understandable, when you place them alongside some of the positions they're reacting against. While many progressive advocates for gay and lesbian people have joined the fight for the legalization of same-sex marriage, another group of writers and thinkers has suggested that friendship, rather than matrimony, could be the more useful category for thinking about gay partnerships. On this viewpoint, friendship can easily coexist with a sexual relationship. Or, to put it more precisely, a sexual, romantic partnership, such as a gay relationship, can be and ought to be described with the language of friendship. Turning Lewis's conclusions on their head, these thinkers want to suggest that all gay relationships are, at root, species of a wider genus. Eros isn't an alternative to friendship; it's one particular form that friendship can assume.

The British theologian Elizabeth Stuart, for example, has suggested that "a great many lesbian and gay people understand their committed sexual relationships not in terms of marriage or of 'living together' like unmarried heterosexual couples, but in terms of friendship." Drawing on the insights of queer theory and mindful of the problems attending a simple transfer of heterosexual norms and expectations to gay relationships, Stuart and others look to friendship—with its voluntary, nonhierarchical bonds of affection—as a potentially fruitful model for understanding the significance of erotic same-sex partnerships. The result may be, as sociologist Peter Nardi has expressed it, that gay and lesbian people have "elevated friendship to an importance perhaps not matched by any other group." And "friendship," on this view, comes to entail sexual expression.

When you grasp this line of thought, the resultant worries of conservatives like Gerald Bray and Anthony Esolen—that friendship is being blurred and confused with romantic, sexual love, and is thereby disappearing as a legitimate love in its own right—become more intelligible. In reaction to what we might call the sexualization of friendship, Bray, Esolen, and, before them, C. S. Lewis in his own way, were seeking to preserve friendship's integrity on its own terms. Friendship is *not* to be confused with eroticism, they say. Although cultural shifts may have made it all but impossible to conceive of it that way, Christians have a stake in trying to rescue friendship from getting mixed up with romance. Or so goes the argument.

ဆ

But back to where I started. If Lewis, Bray, Esolen, and others are right about friendship, where does that leave someone like my friend Conor? Conor is gay—he has virtually exclusive, and apparently deep-seated and pervasive, erotic feelings and inclinations for men. And Conor is also a serious, thoughtful Christian. He knows he needs friendship, but for him, the people with whom he's likely to form deep and meaningful friendships—that is to say, men his age—are also the people for whom he's most likely to have romantic attractions. What is Conor supposed to do, then? Should he hold himself aloof from close friendships? Should he dive into them with abandon, not caring what may happen sexually as a result? Or is there some other option for Conor?

One way of interpreting his desire is to treat it as something that arose in his life precisely *because of* a lack of male friendship. On this reading, the reason Conor finds himself to be gay, the reason he has sexual feelings for men, rather than a nonsexual, nonromantic desire to be "just good friends" with men, is because he never experienced the kind of deep male affirmation and chaste affection that he needed in his childhood and adolescence. Elizabeth Moberly, who was one of the earliest Christians to advocate the possibility of "changing" one's homosexual orientation, was also one of the first to suggest this line of thought. In her influential 1983 book *Homosexuality: A New Christian Ethic*, Moberly concluded:

> Homosexuality is the kind of problem that needs to be solved
> through relationships. The solution to same-sex deficits is to be
> sought through the medium of one or more non-sexual relation-
> ships with members of the same sex. . . . The male homosexual
> needs a male helper, and the female homosexual a female helper.

And the testimonies that result from adopting Moberly's
perspective often sound something like this: "My homosexual
desires began to fade away as I reconnected with my own gender
through close but nonsexual friendships with other men." In
other words, the reason someone like Conor is gay is because
he hasn't been loved enough by men.

When I mentioned this to Conor, we both agreed that, in light
of our experiences, it was a baffling way to talk about being
gay. We both grew up with fathers who stayed married to our
mothers and sought to know us and care for us. Imperfectly
and yet consistently, they gave us healthy parental love, and we
reciprocated. Moreover, our adolescent years weren't friendless.
I've already mentioned my fellow church youth group friends,
with whom I spent many a weekend camping in the woods and
feeling very affirmed in my masculinity. If you had asked me
in high school if I was suffering from a deficit of male friendship, I might have talked about being "different," somehow,
from my friends. But in the next breath, I would have told you
that when you're going camping with strong guys who listen to
Rachmaninoff and read Keats on the days they're not spelunk-
ing, as I was, it's relatively easy to feel like you have a place in
their world. And Conor agreed. His problem wasn't that his
only friends were girls or that he doubted his manhood; his
problem was that he was *too* close to his male friends—so close
that he, still being in the closet and spending loads of time with
them, pretending to be straight, found himself always pining
for more intimacy than they wanted or knew how to give. His
problem wasn't too little friendship but too much, too deep.

Furthermore, when Conor and I, prior to our meeting, had each decided to investigate the outcomes for people who had tried to eradicate their same-sex desires through close same-sex friendships, we found that those results were meager. Reparative therapy, in various guises, seems to have led to at least some significant change for some; but for many others, it has led to bitter disappointment and the especially poignant suffering of being considered a person "of little faith." For every success story, there seem to be a dozen others who testify to no real shift in their sexual orientation—to the point that the leader of the best known "ex-gay" organization in North America recently said, just prior to closing its doors for good, "The majority of people I have met, and I would say the majority meaning 99.9% of them, have not experienced a change in their orientation." (Or, in the more precise terms of the Stanton Jones and Mark Yarhouse longitudinal study of "sexual orientation change efforts," fourteen of ninety-seven subjects self-reported "successful 'conversion' to heterosexual orientation," meaning, "Most of the individuals who reported that they were heterosexual . . . did not report themselves to be without experience of homosexual arousal, and did not report heterosexual orientation to be unequivocal and uncomplicated.") In short, it seemed unlikely that Conor or I would ever find so much chaste male friendship that our being gay would fade away for good. And that left us back where we began. If we couldn't eradicate our homosexuality, and if we couldn't, therefore, entirely separate out our romantic attractions to men from our desire to be friends with men, then were we simply in a situation that meant we would never experience real friendship—friendship, that is, unalloyed with erotic feelings? Were we doubly doomed—barred from seeking closeness with men, but also held back, due to our own lack of desire, from seeking intimate relationships with women? What were we supposed to do?

For all his unappealing bluster about the dangers of confusing friendship with eros in his essay in *The Four Loves*, it was actually C. S. Lewis who helped me find a way out of this dilemma. His 1960 essay on friendship isn't the only thing Lewis had to say on these matters, and looking elsewhere in his writings has the potential, I now think, to change the way we approach the questions facing gay Christians in the church today.

Consider, for instance, a letter Lewis wrote to a young man named Sheldon Vanauken in 1954. Shortly after he had become a Christian, Sheldon and his wife, Davy, were leading a Bible study for skeptics and other newly converted believers. Sheldon wrote to Lewis to ask for advice about what Christians ought to think about homosexuality. At least two members of Sheldon and Davy's Bible study had come privately to each of them to talk about the matter, and neither Sheldon nor Davy was sure how to reply. Lewis wrote back:

> Our speculations on the cause of the abnormality are not what matters and we must be content with ignorance. The disciples were not told *why* (in terms of efficient cause) the man was born blind (Jn. IX 1–3): only the final cause, that the works of God [should] be made manifest in him. This suggests that in homosexuality, as in every other tribulation, those works can be made manifest: i.e. that every disability conceals a vocation, if only we can find it, [which] will "turn the necessity to glorious gain." Of course, the first step must be to accept any privations [which], if so disabled, we can't lawfully get. The [homosexual] has to accept sexual abstinence just as the poor man has to forego otherwise lawful pleasures because he [would] be unjust to his wife and children if he took them. That is merely a negative condition. [But what should] the positive life of the [homosexual] be?

Setting aside the complications that come with speaking of homosexuality as an "abnormality" and "disability," notice what

Lewis achieves in this letter. First, in contrast to books like Elizabeth Moberly's, Lewis professes ignorance about what causes some people rather than others to develop same-sex attractions. He deliberately avoids a one-size-fits-all approach, comparing gay people's situation to that of the man born blind in the Gospel of John: both find themselves with an unchosen condition over which they have no direct power, and both find that this condition has led to pain.

Second, Lewis doesn't, at least in this letter, envision an easy "fix" for homosexuality. Having mentioned a healing story from the Gospels, it would have been very easy for Lewis to draw a parallel between the blind man's regaining his sight and a contemporary gay Christian's regaining her (allegedly native and original) heterosexual desire. But Lewis doesn't do that. Instead, he talks about sexual asceticism and self-discipline. He speaks of "accepting privations," "abstinence," and "foregoing pleasures," rather than achieving heterosexual functioning or finding psychological "healing."

Third, and most important, he puts his finger on an ancient Christian conviction—that whatever renunciations the Christian life involves can never be the final word. Rather, yielding up one thing—gay sex, in this case—is always about the embrace of another. A loss or a place of pain becomes a gateway into a greater benefit that one wouldn't have been able to find without the loss and pain. And that benefit is best described as a "vocation," a calling and a divinely given commission, to make one's loss and pain a means of service to others.

In all these ways, Lewis gestures toward a way of thinking about what it means to be gay and Christian that requires gay people to ask of themselves: What am I being called *to*, positively? Or, even more pointedly, how might my being gay itself constitute a call, and how might it be the very means by which I discover new ways to love God and others? As soon as you start asking these questions, you may end up saying the sorts of things Lewis goes on to hint at in his letter to Sheldon Vanauken—that perhaps "there [are] certain kinds of sympathy and understanding, a certain social role which mere *men* and mere *women* [could] not give" that are open to gay and lesbian Christians. Perhaps celibate gay and lesbian Christians, precisely in and out of their celibacy, are called to express, rather than simply renounce and deny, same-sex love. And perhaps this is where, for all the potential trials and temptations that come with this way of thinking, same-sex friendship represents one way for gay Christians who wish to be celibate to say: "I am embracing a positive calling. I am, along with every other Christian, called to love and be loved."

Taking this route does require retooling the vision of friendship that Lewis outlines in *The Four Loves*. You can't very well commit yourself to pursuing chaste same-sex friendship as a gay Christian and expect that romantic, erotic feelings won't, somehow, be involved in that pursuit. The British theologian Janet Martin Soskice parodies the neatly circumscribed version of friendship Lewis had sketched earlier in *The Four Loves*, in which he had described "an affair of disentangled, or stripped, minds." "How," Soskice wonders, "would Lewis react if another 'stripped mind' arrived at the club and told him that his child had been knocked off a bicycle and was mortally ill? Blustering silence?—'terribly sorry, old boy, didn't know you were married—had offspring—that sort of thing . . . but let's get on with translating Beowulf.'"[2] Soskice is caricaturing, of course, but still, her response highlights how far Lewis's vision of friendship is from the way many of us actually experience friendship. Many of us don't find "love" and "friendship" easily distinguishable,

2. Compare these remarks from Craig A. Williams: "Although they invite being read as universally valid statements, formulations like [Lewis's] in fact speak to a specifically English male experience of friendship—taciturn, understated, indirect, shy—which in some other cultural spheres would seem peculiar at best, barely worthy of the name of friendship at worst."

nor—even if we're straight—are we always able to tell where longings for same-sex closeness and desires for companionship and company begin and end. More often, these realities shade into one another, coloring and texturing our experience of friendship in complex ways.

Fortunately, Lewis can be of help here too. Elsewhere, outside his essay on friendship, he demonstrates that his own practice of friendship was considerably murkier than the clean demarcations found in *The Four Loves* would suggest. If, in that essay, Lewis suggests that friends are always standing shoulder to shoulder, and never yearning to behold each other's faces and get to know one another's personal histories and hopes and fears, he never quite managed, perhaps, to practice such a disinterested friendship himself. Consider, for instance, his relationship with his oldest and probably dearest friend, Arthur Greeves. The two met when they were boys and bonded over a shared love of Norse mythology. "Many thousands of people," Lewis would later write, "have had the experience of finding the first friend, and it is none the less a wonder; as great a wonder (*pace* the novelists) as first love, or even a greater." For the next several decades, until the end of Lewis's life, the two would maintain their friendship in spite of geographical distance, a gap in intellectual aptitude, and other trivial and not-so-trivial differences and disagreements.

Arthur Greeves admitted at some point to Lewis that he was a homosexual. But as far as the textual record goes, there is no evidence that this ever proved to be an impediment to their intimacy. Lewis certainly didn't try to distance himself from Greeves on account of it, as if he needed to hold himself aloof from Greeves's complex feelings—which may, in any case, never have been directed toward Lewis at all—in order to keep himself from learning too much about his friend's personal life. On the contrary, their letters are filled with the sort of intimate exchanges that, in the terms set by *The Four Loves*, could only be described as "entangled," not "stripped."

In what turned out to be the final year of Lewis's life, he was planning a holiday with Greeves in Ireland. When a heart attack prevented Lewis from keeping those plans, he wrote in the final letter he ever sent to Greeves, "It looks as if you and I shall never meet again in this life. This often saddens me [very] much." And then, in the letter's last line, "Oh Arthur, never to see you again!" If Lewis wanted friendship to be defined solely in terms of shared interests and never in terms of an emotional enmeshment of personalities, he didn't succeed with Greeves. Their letters, in fact, still serve as a model for what friendship between a gay man and a heterosexual sympathizer and confidant might become: frequent in contact, reciprocally self-disclosing, laced with humor, and heightened with long familiarity. In short, Lewis himself in his letters to Greeves sowed the seeds for a critique of what he would later come to write in *The Four Loves* about the necessity for friendship and romantic attraction to be held rigidly apart.

ॐ

In my experience, the question isn't so much whether my male friendships will involve some sort of romantic attraction. The question is how they will do so, and how my friends and I will choose to respond to or negotiate that reality when it appears.

Admittedly, I share Gerald Bray and Anthony Esolen's worries about the legitimation of same-sex sexual partnerships in the Christian church. I, too, am convinced that such partnerships are outside the bounds of God's will for human flourishing. They cut against the grain of God's hallowing of male and female as the marital unit—a covenantal bond ordered toward the bearing and raising of children and, together with the corresponding Christian vocation of celibacy, signifying Christ's love for the church. But in a way that Bray and Esolen seem not to consider viable, I also want to explore the way my same-sex attractions are inescapably bound up with my gift for and calling to friendship. My question, at root, is how I can steward and sanctify my homosexual orientation in such a way that it can be a doorway to blessing and grace.

For my part, living with this question has meant cultivating greater self-awareness. I've had to learn to face, rather than run away from, the attractions I've developed for certain male friends over the years. I have not only had to learn to admit these feelings to myself, to see them for what they are and acknowledge their complexity, but I have also had to find appropriate confessors and wise pastoral guides who can listen to me and help me tease out the significance of what I'm feeling.

I remember, for instance, confiding to a pastor a sexual attraction that I had for a friend. He listened patiently and helped me see my way forward more clearly. Months later, though, as I made plans to move away, that pastor told me, "Wes, *when* you fall in love with someone again—notice I say *when*, not *if*—then please know that you're welcome to call me, and we can talk through this together. And," he added, "I hope you will find someone who's there in your own church with whom you can talk about these things too." The sober, confident realism of these words cheered me. My pastor gave me permission to own my sexuality and at the same time not keep myself quarantined from any possible experience of romantic love (as if such a thing were possible, even in cloistered conditions). But his words also assured me, implicitly, that I needed accountability. I needed to continue to nurture my own self-knowledge, to become familiar with my patterns of desire and my temptations to dissemble, even in the privacy of my own thoughts. And I also needed to find trusted counselors—priests, spiritual directors, and therapists, if need be—who could serve as my sounding boards and reality checks, making sure I wasn't allowing myself to rationalize immature, irresponsible sexual behavior in my quest to find deep friendship.

More than that, though, I also needed to cultivate another, related kind of self-awareness. I needed to explore how my being gay might involve what a thoughtful friend of mine has called a special "genius for friendship." *Genius* doesn't just mean intellectual aptitude or brilliance; it can equally refer to a talent, a knack, a particular flair for something, or a certain kind of practical wisdom, so that we say things like, "He's a genius when it comes to baking cakes," or "She's a tightrope-walking genius." Might there be, my friend asked, a way in which gay people have, whether by natural inclinations or through childhood trial and error or some combination of the two (among other factors), a sort of enviable insight into how to foster and enhance same-sex friendships? If so, part of this may be owing to the skills gay kids have to learn if they plan to survive middle school: skills of self-restraint and creative resolution when they develop a crush on their best friend, self-control in speech and action as they try to navigate such a tricky situation without cutting themselves off from relationships, and balance and delicacy in tending relationships even when they retain their potential for messiness.

Despite what you might conclude from cultural sound bites, being gay isn't only, or even primarily, about what people choose to do in bed. Even for straight people, sexuality is broader and more mysteriously elusive than that. While it can't be reduced simply to a generic impulse for relationships of any kind, which would render it synonymous with "relationality" or "capacity for companionship," sexuality also shouldn't be abbreviated as "whatever we do with our genitals."

In my experience, at least, being gay colors everything about me, even though I'm celibate. It's less a separable piece of my experience, like a shelf in my office, which is distinguishable from the other shelves, and more like the proverbial drop of ink in a glass of water: not identical with the water, but also not entirely distinct from it either. Being gay is, for me, as much a sensibility as anything else: a heightened sensitivity to and passion for same-sex beauty that helps determine the kind of conversations I have, which people I'm drawn to spend time with, what novels and poems and films I enjoy, the particular visual art I appreciate, and also, I think, the kind of friendships I pursue and try to strengthen. I don't imagine I would have invested half as much effort in loving my male friends, and making sacrifices of time, energy, and even money on their behalf, if I weren't gay. My sexuality, my basic erotic orientation to the world, is inescapably intertwined with how I go about finding and keeping friends.

And for that reason, in light of these experiences, I'm inclined to say that my sexuality can be seen as one of the things, to borrow Lewis's category, that conceals a vocation for me. My sexuality, fallen and easily misused though I take it to be, may lead, nonetheless, to an invitation. Rather than interpreting my sexuality as a license to go to bed with someone or even to form a monogamous sexual partnership with him, I can harness and guide its energies in the direction of sexually abstinent, yet intimate, friendship. Being gay can lead to being chaste, just as being straight can. We hear so much about the hookup culture and various other forms of promiscuity among straight people, but heterosexuality can just as well be expressed in chivalry or even celibacy. And something parallel is true for gay people. My being gay and saying no to gay sex may lead me to be *more* of a friend to men, not less.

ℬ

It's not just me, though, who has to find a way to channel (or "sublimate," to use the clinical term) my longings for same-sex intimacy in the direction of chaste friendship. Pursuing friendship in this form also requires a great appreciation for complexity on the part of my friends themselves. *They* have to be committed to my vocation as much as I am, if we hope to make a long-term friendship work.

I remember talking to the priest I mentioned at the start of this book, the one who instructed me for confirmation in the Church of England, about these things, and she said something along these lines that startled me with its frankness. Not only did *I* have to be circumspect and make sure I maintained appropriate boundaries and safeguards in my pursuit of intimacy, but I also had to find male friends who wouldn't mind the challenges that come when a friend like me is attracted to them. "Wes, we need Christians who won't freak out when their gay friends develop crushes on them," my priest friend said, smiling seriously at her recognition of the difficulty of what she was putting her finger on. "We need men in our churches who are brave enough to be made aware of those attractions and not run away." Nothing about this kind of situation is straightforward or easily resolved. But then again, my priest concluded, since when have Christians ever believed in playing it safe?

℃

On that afternoon in Minneapolis, I told Conor what my priest had said. And as we packed up the leftovers of our lunches and prepared to hike back to the car, I told him too about A. E. Housman.

Near the climax of Tom Stoppard's play about Housman, *The Invention of Love*, the poet is forced to confront what he thought he'd safely concealed: his love for his best friend, Moses Jackson, who is—to borrow the anachronism—"straight." In the room they share together, Housman and Jackson are both sitting down at a table at the end of a day, chatting casually. Out of nowhere, Jackson says to Housman, speaking on behalf of his fiancée, "She thinks you're sweet on me." The air crackles. Housman and Jackson have just been blabbing on about poetry and Latin, taking nothing very seriously. And then, suddenly, this bombshell.

"What?" Housman rasps after a too-long pause.

"Rosa said you're sweet on me," Jackson repeats the words slowly, making sure Housman has heard them so that he'll have to respond.

The dialogue continues, sputtering. Housman tries to evade the charge with good-humored protests. But finally he succumbs. He admits that Rosa is right. "Did you really not know even for a minute?" he asks Jackson.

"How could I know? You seem just like . . . you know, normal."

But what happens next is unexpected: Jackson—somewhat oafishly, awkwardly, and yet in determination not to lose Housman—says, "It's not your fault. That's what I say. It's terrible but it's not your fault. You won't find me casting the first stone." And then: "We'll be just like before." We'll remain friends, he says. Nothing has to change.

Jackson even thinks of practicalities, for after he's married Rosa: "You'll easily find some decent digs round here—we'll catch the same train to work as always, and I bet before you know it you'll meet the right girl. . . . What about that?"

This exchange recalls an earlier scene in the play that I mentioned in a previous chapter, in which Housman, twenty-something at the time, meets his departed self who now dwells among the dead. The dialogue between the two Housmans—the younger, remember, is "Housman," and the older is "AEH"—revolves around how to understand *amicitia*, friendship, the ancient ideal of battlefield comrades. Housman is taken with it. And that's when he utters that line, "I would be such a friend to someone."

But AEH takes the cynical view. "Love," he says to Housman, "will not be deflected from its mischief by being called comradeship or anything else." Try to dress up your feelings as the noble desire to lay down your life for your fellow soldier. Try to persuade yourself that what you feel isn't eros, it's only *philia*. All such disguises will betray you in the end. "Love," AEH says, quoting Sophocles, "is like the ice held in the hand by children. A piece of ice held fast in the fist."

Like a wedge of cold, brilliant crystal, the love you grasp will sear your skin. You'll want to escape the pain. And before you know it, you'll be staring at a hand shiny with moistness, but the ice will be nowhere in sight. First pain, then futility. The disappearance of friendship. You'll read that line from Sophocles and think, *That's the perfect description of trying to love your best friend when he doesn't love you back, or at least not in the way you wish he would.*

"Love it is, then," says Housman, somewhat ruefully. "I will make the best of it."

Perhaps, in the end, that determination to make the best of a complex, fraught set of circumstances is where those of us who are Christian, gay, and committed to celibacy all find ourselves, sooner or later. That's what I said to Conor that afternoon we spent together.

I don't imagine that falling in love with your best friend was any easier for Housman or Jackson than it was for Conor and his closest friend. But what still captivates my imagination, even now, in this brief, aching scene tucked away near the finale of Stoppard's play, are the possibilities it suggests for our lives, Conor's and mine and others too. Could the pain of Housman's affection and the tenderness of Jackson's reply conceal, for these characters, their vocation to love each other, even at great cost? Could Conor's having fallen in love with his best friend become a doorway into greater, spiritual, chaste love, somehow? We won't know, I suspect, until we try to live in such a way that answers yes.

5

Friendship Is a Call to Suffer

Easy at first, the language of friendship
Is, as we soon discover,
Very difficult to speak well. . . .

—W. H. Auden

The more friendship there is, the more tears there will be.

—Pavel Florensky

One is prepared for friendship, not for friends. . . . Friends
are strange: they disappear.

—Roberto Bolaño

I was sitting at my desk waiting for the phone call.
Yesterday, I had asked for this call. "Be sure to call me
and let me know how it goes," I had said to my friend.
That morning he had said to me, "I'm going to talk to her
tonight." He would take her out for dinner, tell her how he felt.

They would verbalize what had been till that point left unsaid but which was obvious to anyone who knew them: that they liked each other, that they wanted to be together. I had known this was coming. I had told myself and told him I was happy about it, that it made me smile to think of them as a couple. "You have to call me immediately," I had said. "I want to hear how it goes."

He called. My stomach seized up. I was not expecting that visceral reaction. *Why am I getting a lump in my throat?*

"Wes," he said. I could hear the grin he couldn't suppress.

My voice was suddenly quavery, cracking. *Hide that*, I thought. "How's it going?" I said, willing cheerfulness. I didn't think he heard the concealed croak. I was surprising myself with my unsteady emotions. *I thought I was prepared for this.*

"Good," he said.

"How was last night?" *I sound happy*, I thought.

"Yeah, good," he said. "We talked. And we both feel the same way. We talked about being together. We're both really happy about it. We like each other." He laughed. He was smiling.

The conversation trailed off. We talked about what we'd each do that night, what work we had left for the afternoon. We said good-bye.

I was unprepared for what happened next. My hands were shaking as I placed the phone on the desk. And the tears came almost immediately. I knelt down and folded my knees under my stomach. Gripping the side of the bed, I sobbed. My eyes stung, I cried so much.

The next day I stepped into the shower. I couldn't stop crying. I covered my face with my hands, feeling the hot water cascading over my fingers, seeping in with the tears.

I got dressed, walked into town. I didn't know what to do with myself. In line at the coffee shop, I felt numb, hearing the faint ring that lingers after a detonation. As soon as I placed my order, I turned away quickly because the tears were back, surging, spilling. Quickly I crossed the room to the staircase, hoping no one was watching. I pulled off my glasses, which were foggy from the heat of the crying. I pressed my thumbs into the corners of my eyes and tried to regain composure.

ℭ

Over the previous several years, my friend and I had become especially close. We liked each other from the time of our first meeting, and our friendship had deepened through many evenings spent talking late into the night. *I have never had a friend who loved me so deeply, or whom I've loved so much,* I frequently thought, although it's a sappy thing to say to yourself, and I shook my head at my own sappiness as I thought it and as I thought of him, and I grinned at my good luck to be loved like this.

This felt like an undoing of that love, and I shook my head at that too, telling myself, "No, I shouldn't feel this way, shouldn't feel sad. I should be happy for them. It's now the *three* of us who are best friends. I haven't lost a friend, I've *gained* one." But in spite of my protestations to myself, it did feel like loss. It felt like my best friend was being taken away, like the boat was shoving off from the dock, and the rope was fraying my fingers as it whipped through my hands and splashed in the water.

A few nights later my friend came over to my apartment. We hadn't spoken for the past two days, since that phone call. Several times I had picked up my cell to call him but had decided against it at the last second. *Too pathetic*, I told myself. But the third day, he came over.

I made a pizza, opened a bottle of wine. We watched a couple of YouTube videos as we ate. We laughed. It felt like it used to feel, before the eternity of the last forty-eight hours. I forgot that she existed, that she was in his life now, that things were different.

After the pizza was gone, there were silences. I didn't know what to do with my hands. I moved them from my crumpled napkin to the back of my chair, then back, sweaty-palmed, to the table.

"Wes, how are you?" my friend said, and in a fraction of an instant, as if a fuse had blown and the room were plunged into blackness, I started to cry. I clenched my fists and swallowed and gritted my teeth, imploring myself to stop. I didn't want him to see how difficult this was, how I felt as though I'd lost all equilibrium, how I'd never felt so unsteady and sad and bereft. But I couldn't stop, and I hid my face in my hands and kept crying. My body was heaving, and I thought, *I've heard people talking about "heaving sobs" and this is what they feel like. This is what it's like when the floodgates inside are opened up and your body is kind of swept along in the tide of it.*

He placed his hand on my knee and held it there. I sensed that his eyes were averted, and I thought I heard him murmur something. And I couldn't stop crying.

At some point, we both stood up, and my friend gave me a long hug, cradling my still-shaking upper body in his arms, and I put my wet face on his shoulder, and he said, "I'm not walking away from you. I'm not leaving. You're not losing me."

The next day I stayed in bed, unable to summon the energy to leave the apartment.

&

Sometime the next week I checked my email and saw that an old friend would be in the area for a visit. He wanted me to come down to where he would be staying and join him for an overnight trip. He wanted to try to find the grave of an old family friend in a nearby cemetery and wondered if I wanted to accompany him. We could go to a cool bar he knew of and take long walks and smoke our pipes in the warm, crickety nighttime air. I sent a reply and said, "Yes, I'll come down," thinking that this would do me good—to get away, to take my mind off things, to get out of town.

The next day I went to put gas in my car, and before I could walk up to the station's front desk to pay, it was like when my dad used to turn on the lawn sprinklers and the water would gurgle and pool around the spinning heads of the sprinkler system before they spurted up—that's what my crying was like, puddling in my hands as I jogged to the bathroom before anyone could see.

The next day I called a long-distance friend. My emotions had scared me with their intensity and abyss-like depths. I told my friend this. She listened with reassuring "mmm's" and "uh-huh's" as I threaded my way back to the beginning, to where I thought the pain started, and I described how I felt like I'd lost my best friend and couldn't get him back, and I was scared this would mean that I'd be alone always, forever. I told her I couldn't imagine finding another friend like this, not in a million years, and therefore I'd end up as a sixty-year-old single man, without children, sitting alone in an apartment somewhere, forlorn, forgotten.

The friend I called, Julie, is a wise woman, one of the wisest I have ever met. She told me about a moment from twenty years ago when she stood on her driveway as her best friend left for language school in Quebec before she moved to Guinea with her husband to be a missionary. "I had been depressed," Julie said, "and she was my lifeline. She held my hand and saw me through it. And now she was leaving, and I didn't know how to cope with that. And all I could do was stand there on the pavement with my arms around her, clinging, and bawl my eyes out."

I gripped the phone as I listened to Julie's story. At one level, it was comforting, knowing she'd been through the same thing. But the comfort was an icy one. It chilled more than it warmed.

&

I am someone who makes sense of life with the help of books. In times of crisis, I'll pile up great stacks of them, looking for comfort and insight. Or, changing the metaphor, books become, in those times especially, the lenses through which I construct meaning out of my experiences, the spectacles through which I view the world. A month or so after my conversation with Julie, I emailed another friend to say that I'd been reading a book that was helping me understand what I was going through. The book's title is *For Fidelity*, and its subtitle—*How Intimacy and Commitment Enrich Our Lives*—with its promise to elucidate what it was I felt I'd lost and couldn't recover, was what drew me to the book in the first place. I included a paragraph from the book in the email:

> Real intimacy, as I am defining it, confronts and discredits the radical individualism of our times by demonstrating the profound importance of human relationships. Just as new life depends upon and arises from sexual union, so the new growth that marks a living personality depends upon discoveries that can only happen within some level of intimate relationship, whether between matrimonial partners or between those dearest of friends who so nearly approximate mates. Without the clean and honest mirrors of intimate friendships, we are lost in that faceless crowd of faces made to meet the faces that they meet, faces designed to remain safely, anonymously conventional.

This captures what my life with my friend was like, I said in the email. When the book talks about "those dearest of friends who so nearly approximate mates"—"mates" here meaning "spouses," I took it—that is exactly the kind of commitment my friend and I enjoyed. The intimacy of which our friendship partook wasn't different in kind from what married partners enjoy; it was more like a different species of the same genus. We were almost married, I thought, so deep was the affection we felt for each other.

I typed out another paragraph from the book and included it in the email too:

> Although matrimonial intimacy is the paradigm of the intimacy that underlies all real community, the fact remains that marriages are different in degree from friendships. . . . We must undress, both emotionally and physically, in order to satisfy our deepest needs for fullest intimacy. But that undressing entails an equally full measure of vulnerability. Thus, complete intimacy cannot develop except within the security or the confidence of a serious and permanent commitment to the relationship. That's the difference in degree between good friends and marriage partners.

I doubted I'd ever read a truer paragraph. Not only did it explain why friendship hadn't satisfied me (it didn't lead to that deepest sort of mutual vulnerability for which marriage vows create a safe context), but it also explained why friendship *could never* satisfy—because it didn't involve "a serious and permanent commitment to the relationship."

Just let a girl come along, I wrote in my email, and watch what happens: the commitment between you and your friend that you thought was serious and permanent purls away like a ribbon of steam from a cup of coffee.

In his reply, my friend said, among other things, "I wonder if, at this point in your life, reading a book with the title *For Fidelity: How Intimacy and Commitment Enrich Our Lives* might be a bit like a woman who struggles with anorexia reading a book on dieting."

Maybe I should lay off the books about fidelity for a while, I decided.

ॐ

I continued to send emails, make phone calls, and video chat with other long-distance friends. Casting lifelines was what I was doing, or reaching for the ones others were casting to me.

My friend and I decided to keep our distance for a few days, to give us both a breather from the intensity, so I wasn't talking with him anymore, at least for the time being.

My friend Patricia, after she first heard my narration of what had happened, wrote:

> Wesley, Wesley. Oh, this is hard. If I were there I would take your face in my hands and put my nose against yours and gently say: stop. Wesley, you've been in love with your friend, as I'm sure you realize. Your heart is broken. Please breathe. You can do this. It has been done by many and I know you can go up this path.

I turned my eyes away from those words, wishing I hadn't read them. *No,* I thought. *No, I don't realize that. I don't realize I've been in love. That's not what this is about.*

A week later I was sitting outdoors eating lunch with the pastor of my church. It was a bright summer day, and we were at a park. The bluebells had begun to fade, but only just. The sun was hot on our faces. I could feel the last of the dew soaking through the canvas of my sneakers.

I asked for this meeting, thinking, *I need to be talking to people here, who are with me face-to-face, who can actually see me and keep an eye on how I'm doing.* I was self-aware enough to know that my emotions were obscuring my vision and that, for the sake of my health, I needed to have a few people who could come over and be with me if things become too overwhelming.

I told my pastor the whole story, starting from when I first met my friend to when I received that fateful phone call.

My pastor was gentle, astute, not given to overstatement or exaggeration. "Wes," he began, and I could tell he was using an intentionally reassuring tone, modulating his voice so as not to alarm me. "It sounds like you've been in love with your friend, and you're trying to pick up the pieces and move on from here. Am I hearing you right?"

I didn't want to say that that was right, because if I did, then wouldn't that mean I would have to give up the relationship? If I admitted, "Yes, I've been in love with him all this time, even though I've tried to hide that fact, even—or especially—from myself," then didn't that mean I was also admitting that the friendship was all wrong? That it had to end?

I wasn't ready for it to end.

ΧϽ

I continued to read books, desperate for assurances that my experience wasn't unique. There was some comfort in knowing that others had been where I was. I recalled that Henri Nouwen, one of my favorite writers even before I discovered that he was also a celibate gay Christian, fell deeply in love with a man as he was moving to accept a permanent staff position at the L'Arche Daybreak community in Toronto to help care for disabled persons. Nouwen was a Catholic priest and had taken vows of celibacy. As far as we know, he kept those vows. But that didn't prevent his falling in love. Nathan was the name of the man for whom Henri developed an affection, and here is what Nouwen writes about the beginning of their relationship in Trosly, France, before the move to Toronto:

> Over the past few months we have gradually come to know each other. I was not aware of how significant our relationship had become until he left for a month to visit his friends and family in Canada. I missed his presence greatly and looked forward to his return.
>
> Two days ago he came back and tonight we went out for supper together. I felt a need to let him know how much I had missed him. I told him that his absence had made me aware of a real affection for him that had grown in me since we had come to know each other. He responded with a strong affirmation of our friendship from his side. As we talked more about past experiences and future plans, it became clear that God had brought

us close for a reason. Nathan hopes to begin theological studies in Toronto in September and plans to live at Daybreak during that time. I am filled with gratitude and joy that God is not only calling me to a new country and a new community, but also offering me a new friendship to make it easier to follow that call.

But all this gratitude and joy eventually gave way to turmoil. In a later journal entry, written months after Nouwen had moved to Daybreak, he recounts in oblique terms the dissolution of his friendship with Nathan:

> As I approached the new life in community, I came to think about my friendship with Nathan as the safe place in the midst of all the transitions and changes. I said to myself, "Well, whatever happens, at least I have a friend to rely on, to go to for support, to be consoled by in hard moments." Somehow I made Nathan the center of my emotional stability and related to the life in community as something I would be able to cope with. In this way my dependence on Nathan prevented me from making the community the true center of my life. Unconsciously I said to myself, "I already have a home. I do not really need another one." As I entered community life more deeply, however, I became gradually aware that the call to follow Jesus unreservedly required me to look for God's guidance more in the common life with handicapped people than in a unique and nurturing friendship.
>
> This discovery created such an excruciating inner pain that it brought me to the edge of despair.

According to Nouwen's biographers, when Nathan realized the real depth of Nouwen's feelings for him, he withdrew. For the first time, Nouwen was forced to recognize what had happened: he had sought friendship and ended up wanting more than the friend was able to give.

When Nouwen finally published his description of what happened, he left out Nathan's name. But you can tell he'd finally owned up to the true character of what he'd felt.

Going to L'Arche and living with very vulnerable people, I had gradually let go of my inner guards and opened my heart more fully to others. Among my many friends, one had been able to touch me in a way I had never been touched before. Our friendship encouraged me to allow myself to be loved and cared for with greater trust and confidence. It was a totally new experience for me, and it brought me immense joy and peace. It seemed as if a door of my interior life had been opened, a door that had remained locked during my youth and most of my adult life.

But this deeply satisfying friendship became the road to my anguish, because soon I discovered that the enormous space that had been opened for me could not be filled by the one who had opened it. I became possessive, needy, and dependent, and when the friendship finally had to be interrupted, I fell apart. I felt abandoned, rejected, and betrayed.

The following months proved to be the darkest in Nouwen's life. He eventually wrote about the place of peace he arrived at, speaking of the "inner voice of love" that he heard at the end of the anguish. It's a picture of rest, of still waters after a squall.

Truthfully, though, that's not the image I took away from reading Nouwen's account and spending time with his biographers. I pictured him instead in his room, alone, receiving the Blessed Sacrament away from the community to which he belonged, unable to meet the gaze of anyone but the priest who tipped the chalice toward his lips. "The body of our Lord Jesus Christ keep you in everlasting life," the priest said, and I pictured Nouwen crying.

I imagined him in his therapist's office, curled in a fetal position. I pictured the therapist, per the regimen they had already agreed on, placing his arms around Nouwen's weeping form and holding him, speaking in hushed tones, "You're safe. You're loved. Your heart is greater than your wounds."

I pictured the alienation, the loneliness.

ℬ

Until the start of this chapter, I have been trying in this book to sketch an attractive, enticing view of friendship. Friendship is a fully honorable love in its own right, I've argued. Friendship is worthy of recognition and celebration, alongside other forms of love like marriage and kinship. Indeed, friendship might even be seen as a kind of kinship itself, strengthened and made more like the love between siblings or spouses. But all that can ring somewhat hollow if you've never had a friendship that approximates that vision, or if you've lost one, in part through your own selfishness and neediness, like I did.

I wish I could say that my friend and I found a way through this tangle of grief and somehow managed to attain an even richer intimacy, but we didn't. I took a job elsewhere, hundreds of miles from where my friend eventually settled, and we each moved on with our lives. For a while, we worked hard to try to stay in touch and remain friends, in spite of the awkwardness of my intensely negative reaction to what, for my friend, was some of the happiest news one could ever report. We tried talking, again, about what had happened, but the collision of my ongoing sense of loss and loneliness with his burgeoning joy at newfound love ultimately proved combustible, and we decided a season of not speaking to each other would be for the best. That season turned into months and then years, and the friendship slowly dwindled.

Now I go whole weeks and months without thinking of my friend's name or remembering what happened between us. But then something will happen—I'll see one of his Facebook posts, or someone will ask me about that season of my life, or a stranger's face will trigger a flood of memories—and it will all come cascading back into mind.

Recently I received an email that had that effect. It was from a friend of mine who wrestles with his own same-sex attraction, and the poignancy and grace with which he expressed his questions immediately took me back to my experience with my friend:

Regardless of what I call myself (bisexual or gay), I *really* do want to experience marital joy, even though I have troubling anxieties and doubts about whether I could achieve the physical or sexual bond with a woman. Based on a deep friendship in graduate school, I am more confident about developing emotional and spiritual intimacy with a woman. When God says "It is not good that man should be alone," I *know* that is true, so true. And I also know that no amount of friendship, hospitality, or service will ever be a substitute for a fitting "helper." It would take a special woman to love me and accept me for who I am. My baggage is heavy. My history is messy. I do not expect my same-sex attraction will ever disappear, but it may very well *diminish* in a healthy, happy, and holy union with a woman. My homosexual disposition will persist as a thorn in my side until the end of my days, but I *imagine* it would be more endurable with a helper than alone. What I cannot imagine, what causes me to wince in terror, is the thought of being celibate in my 40s, 50s, 60s, and beyond. Perhaps I lack your strength or contentment for celibacy. Perhaps I have not experienced the relational support to joyfully pursue a vocation of celibacy. Whatever the case, I'm profoundly restless in my celibacy, so restless that at times I feel like I'm suffocating under the burden of it. Call it weakness, I just need to be needed, and not needed by a friend who closes the distance with a phone call, drive, or flight. I need to be needed by a companion who is there when I return from work, there when I walk in the park, there when I prepare a meal for dinner, there when I read from a book out loud, there when I go to bed, there when I wake up, there when I cry or laugh, there when I am sick. In short, I desire a covenantal relationship where my helper and I witness each other's "moments of being" (Virginia Woolf's lovely expression), otherwise I dread the thought of having those moments forever unwitnessed. Sure, God witnesses my moments of being, but that is not enough. I need the face of God in a watchful and loving human face.

In my reply, I told my friend I knew exactly where he was coming from. Friendship, I said, doesn't solve the problem of loneliness so much as it shifts its coordinates. Just as marriage isn't a magic bullet for the pain of loneliness, neither is friendship. It does, we hope, pull us out of ourselves, orienting our vision to our neighbors. But no, I said, it's not enough. It's never enough.

As I've worked on writing this book, I've become increasingly aware of the need to speak honestly about all the ways friendship can involve significant disappointment, struggle, and failure. "Finding the right way to talk about pain," I told a friend early on in the research stage, "will be the determining ingredient in whether or not my writing will be able to give any hope to readers who want friendships desperately but can't ever seem to find ones that are deep enough to answer their hunger."

I believe in what I've written here so far. I believe that friendship *can* become something much stronger and more robust than what we've often made of it in the modern world. I even believe gay and lesbian Christians who choose celibacy can find friendship to be a form of love they, specifically, are gifted and called to pursue. I believe the lonely can find familial bonds, and I believe in the ideal of spiritual brother- and sisterhood in the church.

And yet the danger is that, believing all those things, I would treat friendship as a kind of panacea, an easy way of mitigating the pain of our various circumstances in a world enthralled with the myths of family, sex, and individualism. "Having trouble feeling fulfilled in celibacy? Here's a great solution to your lack of intimacy and closeness with others—it's called *friendship!*" "Down on your marriage? Not to worry: you, too, can find love and meaning in *friendship!*" The danger is that I'll idealize friendship as a quick fix for loneliness and relational burdens rather than as something requiring substantial burden-bearing itself.

Insofar as there is an answer to this problem, I suspect it lies in the recognition that friendship involves just as much of an ascetic struggle as marriage or parenting or monastic vows or any other form of Christian love. C. S. Lewis wrote the following about charity, but he might equally have written it of friendship: "To love at all is to be vulnerable. Love anything, and your heart will certainly be wrung and possibly be broken. If you want to make sure of keeping it intact, you must give your heart to no one, not even to an animal." The calling of friendship is, in other words, a call to pain. Joy, yes, and consolation, but not as a substitute for pain.

And not only one's own private pain, as I experienced. Friendship is a call to voluntarily take up the pain of others, bearing it with and for them, by virtue of our relation to Christ. Charles Williams, C. S. Lewis's eccentric friend and fellow "Inkling," wrote movingly of this calling of friends to "co-inhere" with one another. As Alan Jacobs explains,

> What Williams desired was to explore the most radical implications of Jesus's commands to "bear one another's burdens" and "weep with those who weep, rejoice with those who rejoice." The "way of exchange," as he often called it—"dying each other's life, living each other's death"—a kind of *moral* economy in which prayer and love are the currency rather than money. ("Money is *a* medium of exchange," he writes in one of his poems.) Williams believed that if a Christian sees another person suffering, it is that Christian's duty to pray to take on that suffering him- or herself: to become, in an almost literally Christ-like act, the vicarious substitute for one's neighbor.

In this picture, there is certainly a call to deep friendship— deeper than most of us ever get around to fathoming. But it

is also simultaneously, on *this* side of God's final restoration
of all things, as much a call to desolation as consolation. It is
a call to share in the pain and suffering of others and thereby
imitate Christ, who bore the burdens of others in his journey
to the cross.

If our churches and communities learn to take friendship
seriously as a genuine love worthy of honor and public recognition—as I hope they will—the result will be, I trust, a
diminishment of all our various forms of isolation and loneliness, but it won't mean the simple cancellation of the price of
suffering. Think of Aelred's favorite scriptural text to quote
when making his case for friendship: "No one has greater love
than this, that someone lays down his life for his friends" (John
15:13, my translation). Friendship here is linked to, or even
defined by, death.

Or consider Jesus's public demonstration of the depth of his
own friendship to Lazarus: he weeps because Lazarus is dead
(John 11:35–36). Or think of John Henry Newman's emphasis
on Jesus's special friendship with his "beloved disciple": the way
that friendship is sealed for eternity is with words spoken from
a cross, the ultimate instrument of suffering and self-surrender
(John 19:26–27).

Friendship, then—for Christians who take their cues from
the arc of the scriptural story—lives with pain. There's the
daily pain of our efforts, as well as our failures, to love each
other under the conditions of sin and weakness that we all
experience, along with the resultant tensions, heartaches, and
losses that such attempts can incur. And, additionally, there's
the final pain of surrendering the beloved friend, and surrendering oneself, to death, whether metaphorical or, eventually,
literal. Friendship, in Christian terms, is all about giving up
oneself for the sake of love and embracing the cost of such
radical loyalty. Friendship, in a word, is cruciform. If Jesus is
the ultimate author and exemplar of friendship, then we can't

fail to remember that his own practice of friendship ended with him strung up on an instrument of imperial torture, made helplessly vulnerable and wracked by grief. Friendship for him wasn't an escape route from self-sacrifice. It was the other way around: self-sacrifice was precisely the way he enacted a life of friendship.

ꝏ

A few years after the loss of the friendship I described in the opening pages of this chapter, I was living in the same place again. By then, I had found new friends, and I had experienced a significant measure of healing. No longer was the grief so raw and debilitating. No longer was the feeling of abandonment and alienation so acute.

One night during Holy Week, a new friend, Joseph, called me. Would I be interested, he asked, in going with him and his wife, Alison, to the Great Easter Vigil service at All Saints Church? "It's one of the treasures of the church year," Joseph said, trying to educate me about what I'd inherited in my newfound home in the Anglican church. And besides, he added, it would finish around 10:00 p.m. on Holy Saturday, leaving us plenty of time to go out to a bar afterward and order margaritas to celebrate the Lord's resurrection. I needed no more arm-twisting. "I'd love to," I said.

As we made our way to the small parish church and emerged onto the same street I had walked several years earlier on the morning after my friend had called me with the news about him and his new girlfriend, I realized something had changed. It wasn't that the pain of that earlier time had entirely dissipated. And yet here I was with people I loved, and who loved me, friends who would eventually ask me to become a godparent to their daughter. And I was there with them at the site of the earlier pain, standing amid its rubble but ready to gather the scattered debris and rebuild.

We parked the car and entered the church, and in a few moments all the lights had been extinguished. In the silent, dense darkness, the Paschal candle was lit.

"The light of Christ," the priest chanted.

"Thanks be to God," we chanted in return.

After a somber intonation of a long train of scriptural stories, beginning with the Genesis creation account and finishing with the gathering of the exiled and dispersed tribes of Israel, we finally encircled the baptismal font and celebrated the spiritual birth of a new infant. The priest dipped a palm frond in the water and shook it over our heads, and we laughed and reaffirmed our own baptismal vows, wiping water droplets from our faces as we did so.

And then, with that, the lights were ablaze, and we passed a basket of noisemakers of all shapes and sizes. The priest shouted, permitting himself, finally, a huge, goofy grin, "Alleluia! Christ is risen!" Together, we shouted in reply, "The Lord is risen indeed! Alleluia!" And we rattled our bells and blew our whistles and sang hymns. I looked at Joseph and Alison as we passed the peace, and their eyes were as bright and happy as I imagined mine were. It had been a long winter, and with our faces and smiles we said to each other, "The night is far gone; the day is at hand." Clapping each other on the back, we embraced.

And then we took Communion. It was the 150th anniversary of the church's founding, and so, breaking tradition, the priest consecrated champagne rather than port. Kneeling at the rail, I missed seeing the usual blood-red in the chalice, but I couldn't dispute that champagne seemed appropriate somehow, not only because of the church's commemoration but also because of my own personal story. The sparkle and fizz spoke of celebration and springtime, of a new chapter beginning right at the place where the old one went wrong. It was a death that we were remembering—the death of God the Son and his blood poured out—but, for us, that death tasted like champagne. The divine self-sacrifice tasted like companionship and laughter and joy.

Later, at a restaurant, we ordered large margaritas. We smiled at each other across the table, feeling lucky and blessed, talking about nothing much in particular and enjoying the last few minutes we had together before Joseph and Alison had to go back and relieve their babysitter. Halfway through the evening, we spilled one of the margaritas across the length of the table, and we laughed some more.

It wasn't exactly the kind of redemption I would have known to hope for or would have imagined. And it certainly didn't resolve all the lingering disappointment and confusion from my broken friendship. But as we drove home, and I watched my old haunts drift by through the car windows, and I remembered walking those streets nearly blinded by my tears just a few years before, I felt a twinge of hope.

Granted, it wasn't earth-shattering. There was no light from heaven or an audible voice of assurance. But it was, at least for that moment, enough.

6

Patterns of the Possible

Vibrant Christian communities where married couples and celibates live side by side in deep friendships could be a powerful countercultural sign, witnessing to the fact—almost unbelievable to many of our contemporaries—that clear limits set to the bodily expression of love do not keep one from finding happiness and fulfillment.

—Brother John of Taizé

The right kind of friendship between us . . . should begin in Christ, be maintained according to Christ, and have its end and value referred to Christ.

—Aelred of Rievaulx

In Jamie O'Neill's luminous novel *At Swim, Two Boys*, the protagonist Jim is in love with his friend Doyler. Living as he does in early twentieth-century Ireland, he knows he can't express that love in the way that he would like to. But he finds some hope in the ancient stories of Greek and Roman friendships, of comrades in arms. Jim

> had grasped instinctively [the] significance [of those tales]: that more than stories, they were patterns of the possible. And I think, how happier my boyhood should have been, had somebody—Listen, boy, listen to my tale—thought to tell me the truth. Listen while I tell you, boy, these men loved and yet were noble. You too shall love, body and soul, as they; and there shall be a place for you, boy, noble and magnificent as any. Hold true to your love: these things shall be.

I have become increasingly drawn to that phrase—that there exist, for someone like Jim, whether he or she is gay or straight, "patterns of the possible." I'm drawn to the idea that, by rediscovering ancient, and not-so-ancient, forms and exemplars of friendship, we all might be able to find the right place to put the love we have to give. That, as O'Neill's novel says, *these things shall be.* Here, at the end of these reflections, I want to try to lay out some of those possible patterns, in the hope that our churches and communities may begin, however haltingly, to embody them.

It's true that friendships of the depth and beauty I've tried to describe aren't easy to come by. The vagaries of our fallen world and our fallen selves are too pervasive, and God's providential grace too elusively mysterious, for any substantial confidence in our own unaided ability to make and preserve friendships. Still, I do want to end with some concrete, specific ways we might nurture hope in friendship's recovery. I believe in the possibility of a renewal of friendship, and here are some ways I think we can hold ourselves open to that possibility. Here are some patterns that more committed, more sibling-like friendships may take.

ℛ

First, following Aelred, we might learn simply to admit—with specificity and unabashed honesty—our need for friendship. In

Spiritual Friendship, Aelred writes, "Those who claim that their lives should be such as to console no one and to be a burden or an occasion of grief to no one, who derive no joy from others' success and inflict no bitterness on others with their own perversity, I would call not human beings but beasts." It is, Aelred means, wonderfully *natural* to need and want friendship. It's what we were created for and intended to pursue, and being a loner goes against the grain of our created nature. Therefore, in the absence of friendship, or when it feels especially tenuous or even eclipsed, part of our task is to learn to articulate, to ourselves and to the communities to which we belong, how that loss affects us. We have to learn to describe what it is we look for when we look for friendship. We have to talk about our particular need for it before we can hope to find the kind of friendship that will speak to that need.

I've already described some of the ways I as a gay Christian feel especially in need of friendship, but I don't assume that I'm an outlier. Other single people, gay or straight or anywhere in between, also need friendship. Married couples with and without children need it, couples who are happily and unhappily married need it, and divorced and widowed people need it too. But—importantly—all these forms of need aren't like identically shaped holes in the puzzle, even though they're looking for the same missing piece. Your need for friendship looks different from mine, and mine from yours. And learning to talk more concretely and more honestly with one another—including our priests, pastors, and small-group leaders—about our particular experiences of wanting friendship has the potential to illumine for us friendship's many-sided magnificence: it answers a range of different needs and, by doing so, reveals more of its intricate beauty.

༄

Second, we might begin to renew the practice of friendship in the church by starting small—with the friendships in which we're already involved. Looking around at the friends we have right now, in the place where we currently find ourselves, even if those friendships are unsatisfying and troubled in various ways, may be the best way to initiate a revival of friendship.

I know well the temptation to think that a better, more exciting friendship lies just around the corner. Like a lover who's more enthralled with the experience of being in love than with the beloved herself, I sometimes fantasize more about friendship than about friends. I remember once sitting down to lunch with two new friends whom I barely knew and thinking, "Could *these* be my new best friends?" Unknowingly, I'd embraced a spiritually harmful form of idealization, seeking the thrill of the chase—the never-ending hunt for the unknown—more than what the poet Jack Gilbert has called "the normal excellence of long accomplishment." And one way of journeying toward a healthier, more sustainable practice of friendship in the church today could be to ask ourselves whom we're already bound to and how we might strengthen *those* bonds. Perhaps, in some cases, this will involve mending a breach or seeking reconciliation. But probably, in more cases, it will simply mean enlivening certain friendships that we've come to take for granted with an infusion of fresh intentionality. We might choose, as a few friends have done with me, to seek a more formal acknowledgment of our friendship by making public promises to each other. Or we might, less dramatically, choose to invite our friends to become more regular fixtures of our lives. This invitation could take a form as unassuming as setting up a regular time of walking the dogs together on Tuesday mornings or walking to the corner coffee shop after dropping the kids off at preschool on Thursdays.

I remember sitting around the table once after dinner with some married friends of mine. They were thinking out loud about their upcoming extended family vacation, and, the next minute, I heard them ask me, "Wes, do you want to join us?"

"Really? I wouldn't be intruding on your family time?" I replied, raising an eyebrow.

"Not at all. We'd love to have you!"

Taking a step toward strengthening a bond of friendship can be as uncomplicated and down-to-earth as that.

&

Third, we could look for ways to remind ourselves that friendship (like many other loves) flourishes best when it's consciously practiced in community with others. Far from hindering our pursuit of friendship, our churches may be exactly the right places to root our friendships and look for their deepening. And, in the process, our friendships may be spared from becoming ingrown and obsessively introspective.

As I narrated in the last chapter, I once placed enormous expectations on one particular friendship. I had thought that this one friend was all I needed, and I spent a majority of waking hours planning how to strengthen and preserve that friendship at all costs. When the friendship eventually collapsed under that pressure, I was, as I've described, inconsolable. In the middle of this trauma, a wise artist friend, John, sent me a triptych he had created for me, along with an original poem.

The middle panel of the art piece is a cropped portion of Caravaggio's portrait of Narcissus, gazing deeply into a watery image of his own face, enthralled with its carefully circumscribed lineaments. Next to it, in the left panel, is a photograph John took of a pool in a stand of trees. The water reflects scraggly branches overhead, and just visible in the lower half of the puddle is John's face. "Other faces, familiar," his accompanying poem says, offering an interpretation of the image. "Yet they come and go, / Momentary flickers of light." Narcissus looks, catches a glimpse of friends he might have held onto, but their reflection is dim, darkened, and, ultimately, vanishing.

But on the right side of the triptych, in the third panel, is an image of a sunset. Silhouetted against the brilliant sky are three birds in flight. That sky, John said to me, is what I might see if I step away from the wooded pool and look up. True, I won't find an image of a pair of friends, eyes locked in mutual affection, and with it the guarantee of an exclusive bond. But in that sight of three I might, John assured me, catch a glimpse of friendship's expansion, friendship's cross-shaped transformation and redemption, that I'd been resisting up to that point.

"Friendship should not be me and the other, but me and you, and the other," said Abbot Notker Wolf. Three birds, dark against the bronzed sky. An image of what friendship can be when we learn to recognize its place in the church. It's an image I came—begrudgingly at first but, over time, gladly—to welcome.

Fourth, we might also learn to embrace the converse of the last point: that our friendships may strengthen our communities. If it's true that communities may spare friendships from becoming too narcissistic and exclusive, it's also true that our friendships may, in turn, spare our communities from becoming too bureaucratic and impersonal. Remember Pavel Florensky's metaphor: friendship is the molecule of the community, holding the church together.

Christian leaders, especially, should keep this in mind. Priests and pastors have a vested interest in their congregations being filled with people who are friends with one another. They should look for ways to encourage the formation and nurture of those friendships. Why not host a congregational retreat with special teaching on the theme of friendship, as my church has done recently? Why not preach a sermon series on friendship or host a Bible study, as I've heard of certain college ministers doing, on the theme? "Lots of Catholic parishes offer special blessings for everything from moms to sore throats; surely friendship is at least as important as streptococcus!" writes Eve Tushnet. Pastors and counselors could pray a blessing on pairs of friends, even in the privacy of their shared apartments or campus residence halls.

But lay people, too, can seize the initiative themselves, regardless of whether their spiritual leaders always understand their particular need for friendship. Once, after I moved to England and found a church to attend, one of the pastors and I met at a service. We had a pleasant enough conversation, and we made plans to meet for coffee later in the week. I still remember seeing Chris walking through the doors of the coffee shop, his hoodie rumpled and his hair slightly unruly, with his messenger bag slung over his shoulder. Looking back, our meeting each other almost seems fortuitous, as if destiny were involved. (Is this a common denominator in all great friendships?) We talked about worship (his role at the church was to lead in music) and theology. As I recall, we spent some time talking about his undergraduate philosophy degree. We talked about America. As an expat, I welcomed his curiosity about a home I was beginning to miss. More than any conversational topic, though, what I recall from that meeting was the kindling of fellow feeling that enlivened us both. We *enjoyed* each other; there was the sort of mutual understanding and appreciation—"Wait, you've thought that too? I didn't know I could find someone who thought so!"— that marks people out as bound for a deeper relationship than most. And this was to do with Chris's being *Chris*. He wasn't substitutable: what made that conversation valuable—and what went on to strengthen a friendship for the years ahead, though I didn't know that at the time—was this person and not another. His unpredictable, up-and-down moods; his vigorous gesticulations (punctuated by that trademark palm-on-the-forehead as he pondered what he wanted to say next); his always-askew hooded sweatshirt; his combination of vibrant, charismatic Christian devotion with a bohemian attraction to the counterculture; the sunray flash of a quick smile and the storm-cloud shadow of a furrowed brow. I came to love *him*.

Then, almost as soon as our friendship had begun, I moved away. I needed a hiatus from graduate school, and I returned to the United States for what I imagined as the foreseeable future. Toward the end of what turned out to be only one year back home, Chris and his wife, Hannah, came to visit me. I lived in Minnesota at the time, and we took walks around Lake Calhoun in a July heat wave. Hannah, playing the tourist with aplomb, wanted to spend time in a Starbucks, which hadn't yet planted its flag in Durham, where she and Chris lived, so we sipped lattes and talked some more.

And a few weeks later, in an unexpected twist, I moved into a terraced house that adjoined theirs, back in Durham, and we became the kind of friends who see each other all the time. Weekly meals, serendipitous drop-ins, shared errands, exchanged favors ("May I borrow an egg?" "You don't happen to have an extra roll of cellotape, do you?"), gifts given (Hannah made me a rose-infused cake for my birthday once, the memory of which still makes my mouth water)—these small ties, each of them nice enough on its own but patterned and substantial when accumulated, became the trellis on which the vines of our relationship gained their health and strength.

It was through this friendship that I found my way into the church where Chris worked. I had been a member there before I met Chris, so it wasn't that he brought me to a place I didn't already belong. But it was through knowing him first, and feeling confident and secure in our mutual affection, that I began to reach out for other friendships with people in the congregation. Through Chris, I got to know Ruth, and through Ruth I became friends with Katherine. And on it went. This, I take it, is something of what Florensky had in mind when he spoke of the bond of friendship as "the properly human element of the Church." Knowing one friend makes another of my fellow church members not just another solitary individual whom I might or might not come to know. Rather, that other church member is, precisely, the friend of my friend. Having friends in the church, we don't simply say, "We are friends." We also open ourselves to our community that acknowledges us: "They are friends." Others, thereby, are invited to witness, bless, and join us in the pursuit of friendship. And the door is opened to community.

For this reason, I'm not inclined to say with Diogenes Allen that it's "important to distinguish friendship from Christian fellowship or *koinōnia*." Allen's concern is legitimate as far as it goes—"People can be perfectly good members of the church and part of its fellowship, and still not be friends"—but at least in my experience, church community, hospitality, spiritual siblinghood, and friendship are concepts that start to overlap with one another and lose their distinctiveness, shading and blurring and becoming confused, the more you try to parse them. ("Better sometimes," says Iris Murdoch, "to remain confused.") The affection I felt for Chris and Hannah led me, with them, into yet more friendships; it would have taken great effort to hold myself back from that forward movement if I'd wanted to try to keep my friendships and my relationships with church members neatly separable. The meals I shared with church people, many of whom I didn't have any obvious natural affinities for, turned—occasionally, gradually—into something remarkably like friendship. You might say, tweaking William Stringfellow, that acquaintance became community, and community led to friendship. Or perhaps it's the other way around: friendship led to community. Either way, I've given up the project of sorting out that particular confusion.

ᏸ

Fifth, and along the same lines, we might begin to imagine some specific ways for our friendships to become doorways to hospitality and welcoming of strangers. Looking back on what I now think of as a few golden years of friendship in Durham, I can see how friendship was both the context for hospitality and also, for me, the result of being welcomed hospitably by others. The pastor of my church and his wife, for instance, were known for regularly inviting any and all kinds of people, including many university students like me whose families lived far away, to have Sunday dinner at their house and spend holidays with them (or even to live with them for extended periods of time). On my first visit to their house, I was struck by how their fourteen-year-old son made a point of initiating conversation with me and was at ease asking thoughtful, open-ended questions. When I later asked him how he'd managed to become so comfortable with young adults and other older guests, he replied that he'd never known a time in his childhood when the family hadn't had an eclectic group of dinner companions around the table. "In fact, it feels weird now when we *don't* have guests around," he said. And he credited those guests, in part, for the vibrancy of his own evangelical faith.

Likewise, another one of the church leaders was a single woman in her early forties. Hosting Sunday dinner parties was part of her regular routine, as well, and as I've often told people, I never saw an even number of chairs around her table. What strikes me, in retrospect, is how easy it would have been for her to have invited mainly other single people to her after-church meals. With other single guests, there would have been more opportunity to talk about common interests and habits, and she certainly could have avoided some of the messes that young children create. But I'm grateful she didn't, because I now have at least one strong, happy memory of it seeming like the most normal thing in the world for a single person to buy a house with a big dining room, make sure that that room is furnished with an extendable table and plenty of extra chairs, and invite people from outside her own life situation to be her guests.

In these ways, among others, I saw friendships leading to habits of hospitality. Friendships were what made it possible for hospitality to be a welcome *into* something. By nurturing friendships, the members of my church guaranteed that when others were invited into their circle, it was precisely that—a warm, loving circle—that people stepped into. And, correspondingly, I saw those overtures of welcome lead to deeper and richer friendships. It was a spiraling movement, in which one thing led to another, that we too, I think, can replicate.

℘

Sixth, we might begin to look for ways to resist the allure of mobility and choose to *stay*—either literally, by remaining physically in the same place, or else spiritually and emotionally, even when love requires costly sacrifices—with our friends.

Starting last year, a group of friends, all of us somehow connected to the seminary where I teach, began to meet every other week for dinner. We would say Compline together, the eighth of the set liturgical "hours," or offices, adapted for Anglicans in the Book of Common Prayer. Then we would uncover the dishes we'd all brought and enjoy a leisurely meal, oohing and ahhing over each other's culinary achievements.

The evenings usually started with someone letting off steam about work-related woes. We would all listen and chip in with our own empathetic anecdotes as we could, leavening the retellings with humor and, occasionally, just the right words of wisdom that pointed out a way forward. Almost always, though, the evenings turned more personal as the hours went by. I remember one night when virtually all of us wept openly as we went around the circle, one by one, and asked each other to remember certain situations, or family members, or hopes, or fears in our prayers. Another night one of the friends, a priest, led us in a service of blessing for my house, a new rental I had moved into largely so that I could be nearer to certain members of this group.

Out of this ragtag dinner band—"The Ambridge Project," we christened ourselves, because of our vision for neighborhood communal living in our town of the same name—deeper friendships emerged, and for me, one of these friendships became especially treasured. Overnight, it seemed, I had grown notably close to two of the group members, a husband and wife named Aidan and Mel. To Thursday-night group dinners we added a regular Monday-night dinner, with just the three of us. And to that, in time, we added a regular Tuesday-night dinner, when I started joining Aidan and Mel and their housemates, another couple, Jamie and Gretchen, at the end of a long teaching day.

But the initial charm of friendship rarely keeps its sparkle, and this one was no exception. Difficulties arose (I'll leave them vague in my retelling here) that reminded us all how quickly circumstances can threaten any optimism about future plans. But right in the middle of these personal setbacks, we hatched a plan. What if the three of us shared a house? Maybe we could even consider adding a fourth member, another single person who had been a regular part of our dinner group. The more we talked, the more this seemed like where all our evenings together had been pointing. We would say with our actions, and not just with our prayer books and our soup pots, that we were a community, that we wanted the unplanned rituals of daily life together to be the building blocks of any future friendship we enjoyed. And so we picked a house that we would rent (mine, as it happened: they would just move in), we settled on a date, and we started imagining things we'd do: where we'd put the guest room, how we'd divvy up the cooking, when we wanted to host the Ambridge Project around our table.

The more we talked, the more I started to hope in the consolations of this friendship. I was careful to remind myself that it was a gift that had emerged suddenly and it could depart just as quickly as it had appeared. Gun-shy from my earlier experience in England, I didn't want to become too emotionally invested and not leave myself an oasis of self-reliance, in case my friends moved away or didn't entirely reciprocate my affection. ("I sometimes worry that my hunger for friendship may be pathological," writes Stanley Hauerwas, in a sentence I could have easily written myself.) But it was too late. Before I had realized what was happening, I had already come to count on my friends for daily companionship and the sort of unassuming, trivial intimacies that often seem to mark the difference between casual acquaintances and trusted confidants: inside jokes and petty gossip, shared leftovers and small favors, like grocery-store runs and airport shuttling, exchanged. Nervous about codependency and wanting to avoid repeating my previous, painful overreliance on one friendship to the exclusion of others, I called a pastor friend of mine and explained the situation. After listening to me fret over the possible dangers and drawbacks of letting myself get too close to Aidan and Mel, he finally said, "Wes, is it possible God has brought these two friends into your life and wants you simply to let them befriend you?"

Shortly before they had planned to move in, a job offer came for Aidan that would require a cross-country move. It had landed suddenly, unforeseen, in his lap, and he wondered whether to take it. He told me the news quietly, aware of how seismic a change this was for all our plans for the upcoming year.

"I'll feel very sad if you go," I said at first, "but of course I'll support you 100 percent if this is what you feel you need to do."

I said those words, but I wasn't prepared for how difficult it became to maintain that support. My disappointment grew and deepened, and I cried a lot.

Finally, on the eve of the day they had to make a decision, Aidan and Mel came over, and we talked. I tried to assure them that, whatever they decided, I would come to terms with it and do my utmost to offer encouragement and happiness and whatever else they might need to make their move as painless as possible. But I also told them that this was hard for me, harder than I'd ever expected it would be, and that I had shed tears over it. "If I had children," I said, "I would ask you two to be godparents. That's how I feel about this friendship."

"I have no idea what we should do," Aidan confessed.

As they left, we hugged one another good-bye, and I promised to pray for their decision. The next day, I checked my phone incessantly.

The previous week, I had had lunch with a gay Christian friend who's several years younger than me. As he described what I've heard a thousand times before from other people in our shoes—that what he feared above all was getting close to people only to have to say good-bye over and over again and remain stuck in a groove of loneliness—I felt an involuntary spasm of compassion for him. I would have said the same things he told me, almost verbatim, when I was his age. As I continued to listen, feelings of pity and sympathy nearly gave me a lump in my throat. Driving home afterward, the thought came to me: *If I feel that way toward this kid whom I barely know, how much more must God feel compassion for me, a son of his who, in his own way, is no less lonely than the young gay man he just had lunch with.* And I felt confident, in that moment, that whatever Aidan and Mel decided about the job offer, somehow or other God would make sure that I was cared for.

The phone call eventually came. "We're staying," they told me. "We're staying in Ambridge."

After so many tears over the past several days, I felt a bizarre mix of emotions in that moment. Initially, of course, there was sheer elation. I would be spending one more year with Aidan and Mel! I could hardly believe my good luck. I also felt happy that, in the course of their making this decision, we had been able to verbalize to one another what our friendship meant to each of us in ways we hadn't hitherto been able to articulate.

On the other hand, I couldn't deny that I felt a pang of guilt. Did I, with my friendship weighing heavily on their minds, cause Aidan and Mel to turn down a once-in-a-lifetime opportunity? Did I also contribute to the complication, or even the derailing, of future career opportunities? And would they feel any resentment toward me, six months from now, say, when the full implications of what they'd done finally dawned on them? None of these complicated feelings have entirely disappeared, though as I write these words the three of us feel newly confident and hopeful that the decision Aidan and Mel made was a good one.

I know we'll see further complications in our friendship down the road. (Communal living is no cakewalk; most of the stories I've heard firsthand about people who have tried it have ended with disappointment.) And I know that, modern life being what it is and with none of us being quite ready to take a vow of stability, we'll likely find ourselves saying a more permanent good-bye at some point in the future, perhaps even as soon as next year. And that will, no doubt, be made even harder after the closeness that comes with sharing a house.

But for now, at least, I feel deeply thankful for what we have. I want to strengthen and nourish it, in whatever creative ways we all can dream up together. I want to receive it as the gift that it is, and I want to be a good steward of it, making it better and richer and deeper however much that's possible.

One night recently, we gathered in our living room to receive a blessing on our friendship from a minister friend of ours. A couple of other friends stood by as witnesses. We cleared the coffee table, and the minister laid out bread and wine for consecration. She began by praying,

> Pour into our hearts, O God, the Holy Spirit's gift of love, that we, clasping each the other's hand, may share the joy of friendship, human and divine, and with your servant Aelred draw many to your community of love; through Jesus Christ

the Righteous, who lives and reigns with you, in the unity of the Holy Spirit, one God, now and forever. Amen.

In front of the coffee table stood an icon of Aelred that Aidan and Mel had recently given to me for Christmas. The abbot was seated, his head haloed, and he held an unfurled scroll in both hands that read, "Friend cleaving to friend in the spirit of Christ." My eyes kept flicking back to Aelred's face as the minister gave a brief homily from Psalm 121, about pilgrims journeying together as friends to the heavenly city. "We have often forgotten friendship in our culture," I remember her saying, "but it *is* worthy of celebration."

Before consecrating the bread and wine, the minister asked the three of us to stand and hold hands. Lifting her own hand and making the sign of the cross, she blessed us. Taking her cue from the historical precedents that Alan Bray's research turned up, she asked for God's protection on our relationships. She asked God to make us faithful companions of one another. None of us could know how long we'd be together in the same place. But she prayed, still, that God would show us how to care for one another in the meantime and how to make our friendship a blessing for others.

Finally, we took Communion together. "The body of Christ, given for you," the minister said. "The blood of Christ, shed for you," the chalice bearer, another friend, said. And then we sang a hymn. Its words spoke of the kind of friendship that only emerges from shared pilgrimage, the sort of that's "born of all we've known together / of Christ's love and agony."

And then we were quiet. The peace of the blessing and the sense of communion lingered in the room, like a whiff of incense. We didn't say anything for a few seconds. The candlelight wavered on the table. We smiled at each other. In that moment, I don't think any of us felt alone.

An Essay on Sources

If you or your church or your small-group Bible study have read this far and are interested in going further in exploring friendship, I would recommend getting ahold of a good survey volume such as Liz Carmichael's *Friendship: Interpreting Christian Love* (London: T&T Clark, 2004) or Paul Wadell's *Becoming Friends: Worship, Justice, and the Practice of Christian Friendship* (Grand Rapids: Brazos, 2002) or, from a more overtly secular point of view, Joseph Epstein's *Friendship: An Exposé* (Boston: Houghton Mifflin, 2006). From there, you could branch out and read Aelred of Rievaulx or C. S. Lewis's classic treatments (see below), before moving on to Samuel Johnson, whose own *practice* of friendship was considerably more positive than some of his comments would suggest. On Johnson, see the lovely essay—which can also double as a fine introduction to the theme at large—"Friendship and Its Discontents," in Alan Jacobs, *A Visit to Vanity Fair: Moral Essays on the Present Age* (Grand Rapids: Brazos, 2001), pp. 71–82.

Another good place to start would be with fiction. Try William Maxwell's plaintive novel *The Folded Leaf* about two adolescent boys or Chaim Potok's gorgeous novels *The Chosen*

(New York: Ballantine, 1967) and *The Promise* (New York: Anchor, 1969), also about adolescent male friendships. Wallace Stegner's *Crossing to Safety* (New York: Random House, 1987) tells the story of a decades-long friendship between two married couples. Gail Caldwell's *Let's Take the Long Way Home: A Memoir of Friendship* (New York: Random House, 2010) is a moving memoir of her friendship with the writer Caroline Knapp, but it reads like a great novel. And of course Tolkien's *The Lord of the Rings* (many editions) and J. K. Rowling's *Harry Potter* series (New York: Scholastic, 2001–11) contain justly popular portrayals of male friendship (and, in the case of Harry Potter, opposite-sex friendship too), as does, I would now add, Donna Tartt's Pulitzer Prize–winning novel *The Goldfinch* (New York: Little, Brown, 2013).

Many writers note that letter collections are the best places to see friendships unfolding. I would agree (see, for instance, C. S. Lewis's correspondence with Arthur Greeves, referenced below), but I'd add that the loveliest writing on friendship I've come across is found in personal essays. Start with Michel de Montaigne, *On Friendship* (trans. M. A. Screech; New York: Penguin, 2005); Andrew Sullivan, "If Love Were All," in *Love Undetectable: Notes on Friendship, Sex, and Survival* (New York: Vintage, 1998), pp. 175–252; and Alan Jacobs, "The End of Friendship," in *Wayfaring: Essays Pleasant and Unpleasant* (Grand Rapids: Eerdmans, 2010), pp. 128–36.

ଚ

The epigraph at the beginning of the book is taken from Alan Bray, *The Friend* (Chicago: University of Chicago Press, 2003), p. 293.

ଚ

The introduction contains the first mention of a book that will come up again several times in the pages that follow: C. S.

Lewis, *The Four Loves* (New York: Harcourt, Brace, 1960). The quote here is taken from page 58. If you're looking for a place to start reading more about friendship, the essay on the theme in this book is as good a place to start as any.

The quote from Eve Tushnet may be found at her old blog, in a post dated February 22, 2011 (http://eve-tushnet.blogspot .com/2011_02_01_archive.html#1023789358054756912, accessed February 24, 2014). And the story of the two friends Jon and Ray is from Mark Slouka, *Brewster: A Novel* (New York: Norton, 2013), pp. 104–5. I owe the reflection on Simon of Cyrene to conversations with Matthew Milliner and Holly Taylor Coolman.

Unless otherwise noted, Bible translations are from the English Standard Version (copyright © 2001 by Crossway Bibles, a division of Good News Publishers. Used by permission. All rights reserved). I have occasionally provided my own translations.

℘

The epigraph in chapter 1 from Digby Anderson is quoted in Joseph Epstein, *Friendship: An Exposé* (p. 64), and the one from Herbert can be found in George Herbert, *The Complete English Works* (Everyman's Library 204; New York: Knopf, 1995), p. 16.

The material from Benjamin Myers came to me via personal correspondence, May 29, 2011. The A. C. Grayling quote in the footnote is from his recent book on the theme, *Friendship* (New Haven: Yale University Press, 2013), p. 3. And Lewis is referenced again, this time from *The Four Loves* (p. 60). I drew the Seth Rogen quote from Joel Stein, "Taking Judd Apatow Seriously" (*Time*, July 31, 2009).

The quote from William Maxwell's novel may be found in *The Folded Leaf* (1959; New York: Vintage Books, 1996), pp. 138–39. And again, if you're looking for reading that might help you follow up themes in my book, I can't recommend this novel too highly.

Niobe Way's book is *Deep Secrets: Boys' Friendships and the Crisis of Connection* (Boston: Harvard University Press, 2011). Compare also William Pollock, *Real Boys: Rescuing Our Sons from the Myths of Boyhood* (New York: Owl Books, 1998), who argues that expecting boys to adhere to a certain masculine script or code doesn't do justice to the complexity of boys' emotional development. I owe the reference to Eric Anderson's research (http://www.bath.ac.uk/news/2010/10/28/anderson/, accessed May 29, 2014) to Aaron Taylor. Carrie English, "A Bridesmaid's Lament" (*Boston Globe*, June 12, 2011) may be found at http://www .boston.com/lifestyle/weddings/articles/2011/06/12/a_brides maids_lament/ (accessed September 21, 2013).

The reference to Cather comes from Willa Cather, *Later Novels* (New York: Library of America, 1990), p. 557. Stephanie Coontz, "How to Stay Married" (*Times* [London], November 30, 2006; http://www.thetimes.co.uk/tto/life/article1724533 .ece, accessed February 3, 2014) provided the quote on older marriage practices and honeymoons. For a fuller account, see Stephanie Coontz, *Marriage, a History: How Love Conquered Marriage* (New York: Penguin, 2005). The quotation from the classicist Craig A. Williams may be found in his *Reading Roman Friendship* (Cambridge: Cambridge University Press, 2012), p. 17.

My book *Washed and Waiting: Reflections on Christian Faithfulness and Homosexuality* (Grand Rapids: Zondervan, 2010) tells the fuller version of my coming to terms with being gay. I lifted the quote from Karl Barth from *Church Dogmatics* IV/2 (Edinburgh: T&T Clark), p. 577. For a discussion of this link—the "Yes" discloses and makes some sense of the "No"—see Christopher C. Roberts, *Creation and Covenant: The Significance of Sexual Difference in the Moral Theology of Marriage* (London: Continuum, 2008), chap. 6; and, especially, Oliver O'Donovan, *Resurrection and Moral Order: An Outline for Evangelical Ethics* (Grand Rapids: Eerdmans, 1986), pp.

67–71. On the bodily resurrection as disclosing the meaning of gender, see Beth Felker Jones, *Marks of His Wounds: Gender Politics and Bodily Resurrection* (Oxford: Oxford University Press, 2007). For my reading of Romans 1, I am most indebted to Simon J. Gathercole, "Sin in God's Economy: Agencies in Romans 1 and 7," in *Divine and Human Agency in Paul and His Cultural Environment*, edited by John M. G. Barclay and Simon J. Gathercole (London: T&T Clark, 2007), pp. 158–72, at pp. 163, 164. Lauren F. Winner's remarkable discussion of loneliness is in *Still: Notes on a Mid-Faith Crisis* (San Francisco: HarperOne, 2012), pp. 57–58.

And, finally, the Tom Stoppard play has been published as *The Invention of Love* (London: Faber and Faber, 1997). If I could pick one text—other than Alan Bray's *The Friend* (about which, more in a moment)—that has shaped the book I've written, it would be this one. For my interpretation of the play, I've relied on conversations with Alan Jacobs and also on my reading of Stoppard's exchange with Daniel Mendelsohn in the *New York Review of Books* (see the August 10, September 21, and October 19, 2000, issues).

ॐ

The epigraphs for chapter 2 come from Diogenes Allen, *Love: Christian Romance, Marriage, Friendship* (1987; Eugene, OR: Wipf & Stock, 2006), p. 43, and G. R. Elton, *Reform and Renewal: Thomas Cromwell and the Common Weal* (Cambridge: Cambridge University Press, 1973), p. 60.

The Bonhoeffer material may be found in Dietrich Bonhoeffer, *Letters and Papers from Prison* (*Dietrich Bonhoeffer Works*, vol. 8; ed. John W. de Gruchy; trans. Isabel Best, Lisa E. Dahill, Reinhard Krauss, and Nancy Lukens; Minneapolis: Fortress, 2010), pp. 224, 247–48, 267, 268. The account of Bethge's later fielding of an audience question is from *The Prison Poems of Dietrich Bonhoeffer*, edited by Edwin Robertson (Guildford,

Surrey: Eagle, 1998), p. 78. For readers wishing to know more about Bonhoeffer's friendship with Bethge and especially its connection to Bonhoeffer's ambiguous sexuality, there is Charles Marsh's splendid, magisterial biography *Strange Glory: A Life of Dietrich Bonhoeffer* (New York: Knopf, 2014). In personal correspondence (April 28, 2014), Marsh told me this about Bonhoeffer's friendship with Bethge: "Frankly I don't know where Bonhoeffer would have ended up had he survived the war. But there is no doubt he was striving for something like a spiritual marriage with Eberhard."

The October 10, 1909, diary entry of Florensky's student, Aleksandr El'chaninov, is quoted in Avril Pyman, *Pavel Florensky: A Quiet Genius* (London: Continuum, 2010), p. 70, and the reference to Florensky's pact with Sergei is mentioned on page 59. For discussion of *adelphōpoiēsis*, a good place to start would be Robin Darling Young, "Gay Marriage: Reimagining Church History," *First Things* (November 1994): 43–48. Pavel Florensky's unconventional "letters" are published as *The Pillar and Ground of the Truth: An Essay in Orthodox Theodicy in Twelve Letters* (trans. Boris Jakim; Princeton: Princeton University Press, 1997), and I have drawn from pages 311, 318, and 326.

The Aelred of Rievaulx quote is taken from one of the other main texts I have grappled with in writing this book—*Spiritual Friendship* (trans. L. C. Braceland; Collegeville, MN: Liturgical Press, 2010); the first quote I mention is found on page 78. I have also lifted quotations from pages 57, 59, and 61. I learned about the stricture against reading Aelred in monasteries from Brian Patrick McGuire, *Friendship and Community: The Monastic Experience, 350–1250* (1988; Ithaca, NY: Cornell University Press, 2010), pp. xliii–xliv. And on Aelred as "gay," see John Boswell, *Christianity, Social Tolerance, and Homosexuality: Gay People in Western Europe from the Beginning of the Christian Era to the Fourteenth Century* (Chicago: University of

Chicago Press, 1980), pp. 222–23. Compare also, though, the discussion in McGuire, *Friendship and Community*, pp. 302–4, which critiques Boswell for greater confidence in his interpretation than Aelred's texts warrant. In the end, however, McGuire agrees that Aelred experienced same-sex attraction: "Insofar as Aelred indicated that he had to cope with a sexual desire for other men, Boswell's interpretation captures one aspect of the special quality of the earlier part of the twelfth century" (p. 303). The "kiss" reference is from Aelred of Rievaulx, *De speculo caritatis*, as quoted in Boswell, *Christianity, Social Tolerance, and Homosexuality*, p. 225.

The first reference to Alan Bray—one of the great heroes of the story I'm telling—is from his "Wedded Friendships," *The Tablet* (August 4, 2001): 8–9, at p. 8. His book is *The Friend* (Chicago: University of Chicago Press, 2003), and I begin by drawing from page 296. I should say, though, that Bray apparently wrote with the hope of promoting the acceptance by the Roman Catholic Church of same-sex marriage. Therefore, as the historian Keith Thomas notes, at times the book "has a tendency to convert speculation into established fact" (*The Ends of Life: Roads to Fulfillment in Early Modern England* [Oxford: Oxford University Press, 2009], p. 344 n. 34). My other quotations from *The Friend* may be found on pages 82, 133, 241, 249. The Florensky quote is again from *The Pillar and Ground of the Truth*, p. 327. I also draw here on Marc Bloch, *Feudal Society*, vol. 1: *The Growth and Ties of Dependence* (2nd ed.; trans. L. A. Manyon; Chicago: University of Chicago Press, 1964), p. 124. The reference to Thomas in the footnote is from *The Ends of Life*, pp. 201–2; a subsequent reference is from page 193.

I also cite Mark Vernon, *The Meaning of Friendship* (Basingstoke, Hampshire: Palgrave Macmillan, 2010), p. 175, and my entire paragraph that quotes from him is indebted to Vernon's discussion. The Michel Foucault quotation is from *Ethics:*

Subjectivity and Truth (*Essential Works of Foucault 1954–1984*, vol. 1; New York: New Press, 1998), p. 171.

Maggie Gallagher's distinction between two kinds of love is from her *Enemies of Eros: How the Sexual Revolution Is Killing Family, Marriage, and Sex and What We Can Do about It* (Los Angeles: Bonus Books, 1989), pp. 240–41. And, again, I reference Bonhoeffer's *Letters and Papers from Prison*, p. 84.

𝅘𝅥

The Paul Wadell epigraph to chapter 3 is from his "Shared Lives: The Challenges of Friendship," *Christian Century*, September 16, 2011; http://www.christiancentury.org/article/2011-08/shared -lives (accessed May 29, 2014).

In my historical discussion, I quote from Steve Summers, *Friendship: Exploring Its Implications for the Church in Postmodernity* (Ecclesiological Investigations; London: T&T Clark, 2009), p. 66, and Homer, *The Iliad* (trans. Richmond Lattimore; Chicago: University of Chicago Press, 1951), 18.81; 19.321–2, 326. My references to Cicero and Aristotle may be found in Cicero, *On Old Age; On Friendship; On Divination* (Loeb Classical Library; Cambridge, MA: Harvard University Press, 1923); *De amicitia* 24 and Aristotle, *Nicomachean Ethics* (Loeb Classical Library; Cambridge, MA: Harvard University Press, 1934), 8.6. A convenient survey of much of the material I'm canvassing here is available in David Konstan, *Friendship in the Classical World* (Cambridge: Cambridge University Press, 1997). The summation of Aristotle is from Gilbert C. Meilaender's remarkably rich *Friendship: A Study in Theological Ethics* (Notre Dame, IN: University of Notre Dame Press, 1981), p. 8, as is the reference to Jeremy Taylor (p. 1) and Samuel Johnson (p. 7). Søren Kierkegaard's closely similar sentiments are from *Works of Love* (trans. Howard and Edna Hong; New York: HarperPerennial, 2009), p. 70; I took the second Kierkegaard quotation from Epstein's *Friendship* (p. 57), mentioned earlier. I quote again from Karl Barth, *Church Dogmatics* IV/2 (Edinburgh: T&T Clark, 1958), p. 819. Gene Outka, *Agape: An Ethical Analysis* (New Haven: Yale University Press, 1972), p. 210, however, cautions against seeing too much continuity between Kierkegaard and Barth here. Unlike Kierkegaard, Barth is "concerned with agape's independence from, not its condemnation of, every relation presupposing liking." I owe this reference in this connection to Alan Jacobs, *A Theology of Reading: The Hermeneutics of Love* (Boulder, CO: Westview, 2001), p. 158 n. 20.

Turning to biblical material, I quote from Summers, *Friendship*, p. 21 again, with added italics. And I turn back to Florensky, *The Pillar and Ground of the Truth*, p. 299. The "political" reading of the David and Jonathan story seems to be the basic import of Robert Alter's comments in his *Ancient Israel* (New York: Norton, 2013), pp. 345, 430. For the "sexual" alternative, see Samuel Terrien, *Till the Heart Sings: A Biblical Theology of Manhood and Womanhood* (Grand Rapids: Eerdmans, 2004), p. 169. My own views have been influenced by Markus Zehnder, "Observations on the Relationship between David and Jonathan and the Debate on Homosexuality," *Westminster Theological Journal* 69 (2007): 127–74, at p. 153.

The "Love wept . . . " sentence is Beth Felker Jones's paraphrase of Alexander Schmemann (Jones, Beth Felker [@bethfelker jones]; "remembering that love is as strong as death and, in the words of Alexander Schmemann, 'Love wept at the grave of his friend,'" Twitter, November 14, 2013, 2:24 p.m.). I draw heavily here from John Henry Newman, "Love of Relations and Friends," in *Parochial and Plain Sermons* (San Francisco: Ignatius, 1997), pp. 259–64, at pp. 259–60. The story about Johnson and Mrs. Knowles is from James Boswell, *The Life of Samuel Johnson* (New York: Penguin, 2008), p. 680.

The judgment of Julie Hanlon Rubio about the Gospels and "family values" is from her valuable treatment *A Christian Theology of Marriage and Family* (Mahwah, NJ: Paulist

Press, 2003), p. 50. I also quote from Paul Griffiths, "Talking with Ahmedinejad," *Christian Century*, October 17, 2006, pp. 8–9, at p. 9. For further reflections on this theme, see Joseph H. Hellerman, *When the Church Was a Family: Recapturing Jesus' Vision for Authentic Christian Community* (Nashville: B&H Academic, 2009), chapter 4. In explicating Paul, I have leaned heavily on Stephen E. Fowl, *Philippians* (Two Horizons New Testament Commentary; Grand Rapids: Eerdmans, 2005), p. 225. The fourth-century Christian author I mention is Paulinus of Nola, who wrote to Pammachius, as quoted in Konstan, *Friendship in the Classical World*, p. 158.

In the next section, I quote from the beautiful book by William Stringfellow, *A Simplicity of Faith: My Experience in Mourning* (Nashville: Abingdon, 1982), p. 48. On John's Gospel, see Sandra Schneiders, *Written That You May Believe: Encountering Jesus in the Fourth Gospel* (New York: Herder & Herder, 2003), p. 194. The Paul D. O'Callaghan quotation I include in the footnote is from *The Feast of Friendship* (Wichita: Eighth Day Press, 2002), p. 54. On the reconfiguration of classical friendship discourse in early Christianity, see, for instance, John Fitzgerald, "Christian Friendship: John, Paul, and the Philippians," *Interpretation* 61 (2007): 284–96; and G. Walter Hansen, *The Letter to the Philippians* (Pillar New Testament Commentary; Grand Rapids: Eerdmans, 2009), who comments: "[Paul] transforms the meaning and experience of friendship by redefining each of the essential ideals of friendship given by Hellenistic essays on friendship in terms of communion with Christ and empowerment by Christ" (p. 11).

I close this chapter with a quote from Lauren F. Winner, *Girl Meets God: A Memoir* (New York: Random House, 2002), p. 188.

&

The epigraphs to chapter 4 are from Christopher C. Roberts, *Creation and Covenant* (p. 227), and *In Defense of Sanity: The*

Best Essays of G. K. Chesterton, edited by Dale Ahlquist, Joseph Pearce, and Aidan Mackey (San Francisco: Ignatius, 2011), p. 33. Matthew Vines's statement was reported in Douglas Quenqua, "Turned Away, He Turned to the Bible," *New York Times*, September 14, 2012; http://www.nytimes.com/2012/09/16/fashion /matthew-vines-wont-rest-in-defending-gay-christians.html (accessed September 23, 2013).

Allan Bloom's lapidary formulation is from his *Love and Friendship* (New York: Simon & Schuster, 1993), p. 281. And here again, I turn to Lewis's *Four Loves* (here pp. 70–71). My comparison of him to Bacon in the footnote relies on Francis Bacon, *The Essayes or Counsels* (Oxford: Oxford University Press, 2000), p. 80. Gerald Bray's worries are available in his "Call to Biblical Values," in *The Way Forward? Christian Voices on Homosexuality and the Church*, edited by Timothy Bradshaw (2nd ed.; Grand Rapids: Eerdmans, 2004), pp. 37–43, at p. 42. For Anthony Esolen's complementary views, I turned to "A Requiem for Friendship: Why Boys Will Not Be Boys and Other Consequences of the Sexual Revolution," *Touchstone* (September 2005): 21–27, at p. 24.

The queer perspective of Elizabeth Stuart is in her book *Just Good Friends: Towards a Lesbian and Gay Theology of Relationships* (London: Mowbray, 1995), p. 28, which is also where I found the reference to Peter Nardi, "That's What Friends Are For: Friends as Family in the Gay and Lesbian Community," in *Modern Homosexualities: Fragments of Lesbian and Gay Experience*, edited by Ken Plummer (London: Routledge, 1992), pp. 108–20, at p. 120. Elizabeth R. Moberly, *Homosexuality: A New Christian Ethic* (Cambridge: Clark, 1983), p. 42, is the groundbreaking "conservative" treatment I mention, and you can see the influence of her views on Chad W. Thompson, *Loving Homosexuals as Jesus Would: A Fresh Christian Approach* (Grand Rapids: Brazos, 2004), p. 125. The reference to the "ex-gay" leader is of course to Alan Chambers, and I found it in Warren Throckmorton, "Alan Chambers: 99.9% Have

Not Experienced a Change in Their Orientation," January 9, 2012, http://wthrockmorton.com/2012/01/alan-chambers-99 -9-have-not-experienced-a-change-in-their-orientation (accessed September 12, 2013). Stanton L. Jones and Mark A. Yarhouse, "A Longitudinal Study of Attempted Religiously Mediated Sexual Orientation Change," *Journal of Sex and Marital Therapy* 37 (2011): 404–27, provided me the precise data on shifts in sexual orientation. Note, however, that even this cautious study relies on self-reporting from a self-selecting group of Christian believers.

Returning to Lewis, I draw on Sheldon Vanauken, *A Severe Mercy* (New York: Harper & Row, 1987), p. 147. The blistering, perhaps unfair, critique from Janet Martin Soskice may be found in her "Friendship," in *Fields of Faith: Theology and Religious Studies for the Twenty-First Century*, edited by David F. Ford, Ben Quash, and Janet Martin Soskice (Cambridge: Cambridge University Press, 2005), pp. 167–81, at p. 172. To complement her perspective, I've again lifted a quotation from Williams, *Reading Roman Friendship*, p. 33. Continuing to explore Lewis's contributions to my theme, I draw on C. S. Lewis, *Surprised by Joy: The Shape of My Early Life* (New York: Harcourt, 1955), pp. 130–31; A. N. Wilson, *C. S. Lewis: A Biography* (New York: Norton, 1990), p. 44; and *The Letters of C. S. Lewis to Arthur Greeves (1914–1963)*, edited by Walter Hooper (New York: Collier, 1979), pp. 565, 566.

Finally, I close the chapter by returning to Stoppard, *The Invention of Love*, pp. 75 and following.

Readers wishing to apply some of the discussions of this chapter to the matter of cross-sex friendships might want to consult Dan Brennan's *Sacred Unions, Sacred Passions: Engaging the Mystery of Friendship between Men and Women* (Elgin, IL: Faith Dance, 2010).

℘

The epigraphs to chapter 5 are from W. H. Auden, "For Friends Only," in his *Collected Poems* (New York: Modern Library, 2007), pp. 705–7, at p. 706; Florensky, *The Pillar and Ground of the Truth*, p. 318; and Roberto Bolaño, *Between Parentheses: Essays, Articles and Speeches, 1998–2003* (trans. Natasha Wimmer; New York: New Directions, 2011), p. 135.

I refer here to Catherine M. Wallace, *For Fidelity: How Intimacy and Commitment Enrich Our Lives* (New York: Vintage, 1999), p. 67; Henri J. M. Nouwen, *The Road to Daybreak: A Spiritual Journey* (New York: Image, 1990), pp. 99, 223; and Henri J. M. Nouwen, *The Inner Voice of Love: A Journey through Anguish to Freedom* (New York: Image, 1999), p. xv. In retelling some of Nouwen's story, I relied on Michael Ford, *Wounded Prophet: A Portrait of Henri J. M. Nouwen* (New York: Doubleday, 2002), and Michael O'Laughlin, *Henri Nouwen: His Life and Vision* (Maryknoll, NY: Orbis, 2005).

Once again, I circle back to Lewis, *The Four Loves* (p. 121), and supplement what he said with reference to one of his fellow "Inklings," Charles Williams, drawing on Alan Jacobs, *The Narnian: The Life and Imagination of C. S. Lewis* (San Francisco: HarperSanFrancisco, 2005), p. 284.

&

I open chapter 6 with two epigraphs, one from Brother John of Taizé, *Friends in Christ: Paths to a New Understanding of the Church* (Maryknoll, NY: Orbis, 2012), pp. 153–54, a book I would highly recommend for those who wish to explore more of the intersection of friendship and community, and one from Aelred, *Spiritual Friendship*, p. 57. A bit later in the chapter, I again quote from *Spiritual Friendship*, p. 82.

I quote from Jamie O'Neill, *At Swim, Two Boys* (New York: Scribner, 2001), pp. 530–31, and Jack Gilbert, *Collected Poems* (New York: Knopf, 2012), p. 28. The quote from Abbot Notker Wolf is found in Summers, *Friendship*, p. 133. The delightful quotation from Tushnet is from my personal correspondence with her on May 15, 2013. Meanwhile, I come back again to Florensky, *The Pillar and Ground of the Truth*, p. 317, this time connecting him with Diogenes Allen's rather different views in his *Love: Christian Romance, Marriage, Friendship*, pp. 58, 60. I steal the Iris Murdoch quip from her *Metaphysics as a Guide to Morals* (New York: Penguin, 1994), p. 147.

The final quote from Stanley Hauerwas is from his memoir *Hannah's Child: A Theologian's Memoir* (Grand Rapids: Eerdmans, 2010), p. 247. And the collect that closes the chapter is from the Episcopal Church's *Lesser Feasts and Fasts* (New York: Church Publishing, 2006), p. 127.

Some of the material in this book was adapted from Wesley Hill, "'Til Death Do Us Part," *Christianity Today* 58/7 (September 2014): 38–44. Used by permission.

Acknowledgments

The idea for this book first came from reading some remarkable work on friendship by Eve Tushnet and Benjamin Myers, who, I am glad to say, have since become friends (and readers of the manuscript!). Their fingerprints are all over these pages, and even if they may disagree with some of the ways I tried to appropriate their insights, I hope they see that I have learned and benefited from their perspectives.

I worked out the initial structure and themes for the book over several thoroughly enjoyable conversations with Alan Jacobs and Brett Foster at the Market Tavern in Durham, England, in the summer of 2011. We met virtually every night for a week in July, and they patiently helped me see what I wanted to accomplish and talked with me about the best way to approach the task. It's gratifying to remember that this book about friendship got its start from these particular friendships. (Alan later read draft chapters and commented extensively.)

I presented some of the material in the book to several audiences and received very useful feedback. I am grateful to audiences at Wheaton College's Wheaton in England program; the True Freedom Trust conference, London; Chawn Hill Church,

Stourbridge, UK; Calvin College; Biola University; the Christian Study Center, Charlottesville, Virginia; Harvard College Faith and Action; my Christian Theology of Friendship class at Trinity School for Ministry, Ambridge, Pennsylvania; St. Stephen's Anglican Church, Sewickley, Pennsylvania; Grace Anglican Church, Slippery Rock, Pennsylvania; and Truett Theological Seminary at Baylor University.

I am also grateful to the crowd at De Spirituali Amicitia, where I floated the very first portions of what became the manuscript. I am also more grateful than I can say to Ron Belgau, my dear friend and comrade in this venture, and our fellow contributors at the Spiritual Friendship blog (spiritualfriendship.org), as well as our commenters, who read and offered feedback on posts that were later modified and included in the book. Matthew Schmitz and R. R. Reno graciously gave us a platform at the First Thoughts blog, where I received more helpful feedback. And if I hadn't participated in the studium on gay Catholic life at the Institute for Church Life at the University of Notre Dame, this book could never have been completed. The camaraderie, provocation, and deep spiritual sustenance I received from that group have been among the greatest blessings of my life. I want to thank Ron especially, and also Sr. Ann Astell, Chris Damian, Joshua Gonnerman, Daniel Hoover, Kyle Keating, Timothy Pisacich, Christopher Roberts, Melinda Selmys, Aaron Taylor, Eve Tushnet, and also John Cavadini for convening us.

I want to thank everyone who talked with me about what I was doing during the writing process, read draft chapters, and in some cases the entire manuscript: Brent Bailey, Kyle Blanchette, Mark Bonnington (and Ruth, Ana, Gus, and Zak Bonnington, as well), Richard Briggs, Betsy Childs, Carrie Frederick Frost, Martha Giltinan, Kathryn Greene-McCreight, Jon and Sarah Hall, Phil Harrold, Steve Holmes, Misty Irons, Matt Jones, Paul Jones, Karen Keen, Timothy Larsen, Stephen Mackereth, Logan Mahan, David Michael (who went above and beyond the call of duty, going through the manuscript with a fine-tooth comb), Matthew Milliner, Walter and Jenny Moberly, Kyler Mulhauser, Jeffrey Murray, Nick Nowalk, Ruth Perrin, Julie Rodgers, Medi Ann Volpe, John Wilson, and Mark Yarhouse.

Working with James Ernest and the team at Brazos Press has been a pleasure from start to finish. I firmly believe I have the best editor in the business. From the beginning, James understood what I was trying to do, and every comment he made was aimed at helping me achieve that goal.

Finally, I want to thank the friends (and their wives, Emily, Hannah, Molly, Megan, Kristi, and Melanie) to whom this book is dedicated. These are people who have embodied what I've written—the ones who have extended to me the kind of friendship that's best described in brotherly, familial, intimate terms: Mike Allen, Chris Juby, David Michael, Abraham Piper, Jono Linebaugh, Orrey McFarland, and Aidan Smith. Soon after I finished the manuscript and told him he was one of the dedicatees, my friend Chris Mitchell passed away. This book is for these friends, and is offered in memory of Chris, with my love.